2015
To my friend,
Bennese, on her
birthday -
Ruth Gauger!

JIMMY & JESSIE
"ABOVE THE CROWD"
A MEMORY OF LOVE

By

RUTH BELL GAUGER

Assisted by Charles King

JIMMY & JESSIE "ABOVE THE CROWD" *A MEMORY OF LOVE*

By
RUTH BELL GAUGER

Assisted by Charles King

Published By:
Timberlane Press
5668 Timberlane Rd.
Bascom, Florida 32423

Printed by:
Brentwood Christian Press
4000 Beallwood Avenue
Columbus, Georgia 31904

CONTENTS

LITERARY DISCLAIMER 5

SPECIAL ACKNOWLEDGMENT 6

ACKNOWLEDGMENTS 7

MILESTONES 8

INTRODUCTION 9

PROLOGUE 12

CHAPTER 1 13

CHAPTER 2 17

CHAPTER 3 22

CHAPTER 4 28

CHAPTER 5 30

CHAPTER 6 33

CHAPTER 7 35

CHAPTER 8 40

CHAPTER 9 50

CHAPTER 10 53

CHAPTER 11 55

CHAPTER 12 58

CHAPTER 13 60

CHAPTER 14 63

CHAPTER 15 66

CHAPTER 16 68

CHAPTER 17 70

CHAPTER 18 71

CHAPTER 19 76

CHAPTER 20 83

CHAPTER 21 85

CHAPTER 22 98

CHAPTER 23 102

CHAPTER 24 104

CHAPTER 25 108

CHAPTER 26 110

EPILOGUE 115

INDEX OF CHARACTERS 116

LITERARY DISCLAIMER

Please be advised that in writing this information to you about the lives of the Walters, Mr. Jimmy and Mrs. Jessie, my purpose is benign and, in no way, means to cast shame or harm upon any person mentioned herein. My motives should be construed as only good and bereft of any ignoble intentions or references to anyone mentioned in this story. Indeed, it is a memory of love dedicated to the heroes of this story, related with adoration and without malice aforethought to anyone.

SPECIAL ACKNOWLEDGMENT

Without the assistance of Charles King, this literary endeavor would be only a memory in my mind -- persistent, yet formless and without ideation.

Declining credit as a coauthor, Charles accepts, instead, acknowledgment for his invaluable assistance in the creation of ideas and the ensuing writing, editing, and publication of this book..

To him, I express my sincere gratitude.

ACKNOWLEDGMENTS

I wish to acknowledge the assistance of the following friends and contributors in the collation and publishing of this literary endeavor:

GEORGE GAUGER

CHARLES HUDSON

LUREE HUDSON

SYLVIA HUTCHINS

HERMAN LARAMORE

AARON (BILLY) McALLISTER

VIRGIL OSWALD

ROBERT ALLEN PEELER

LEO (ROBBIE) ROBINSON

DR. JERRY WINDSOR

MILESTONES

Mr. Jimmy was born November 11, 1902.

Mrs. Jessie was born August 3, 1903.

Mrs. Jessie had one child, William H. Pyke, Jr., known as W. H. Pyke.

Mrs. Jessie met Mr. Jimmy and they were married March 7, 1923.

Mr. Jimmy and Mrs. Jessie became the Walters Duo.

They traveled all over the United States with many different shows and circuses.

They retired in 1934 in the Neal's Landing-Mt. Olive community.

Mrs. Jessie died July 31, 1968.

Mr. Jimmy died in March of 1978.

INTRODUCTION

Dear Reader: This literary effort has not been without many hindrances and disappointments. Initially, I tried to write a simple story about my beloved subjects, Mr. Jimmy and Mrs. Jessie Walters. I had so many ideas and so much information about my subjects; and yet, I was at a complete loss as how to proceed to compile all the information at my disposal into a literary composition that was interesting and informative.

At the outset I wondered about this literary endeavor. I knew it would be a monumental task. How could I, possibly, express to my readers the myriad emotions I wished to convey? My subjects were so far above the realm of the ordinary that I realized any exploitation of their lives and experiences must be revealed in a manner that was truly unusual and bespoke the wonder and joy that I perceived about them.

My queries were answered one day during a conversation with a dear friend of mine, Charles King. I discovered that he would be very interested in a joint effort with me about Mr. Jimmy and Mrs. Jessie.

For this reason, I have enlisted his assistance in this literary undertaking. With a striking ability to express his thoughts and ideas in an articulate and unique manner, Charles has shared his literary talents with me.

Herewith, in a collaborative endeavor with Charles, I present a work of loving memories and anecdotes.

May your delight in reading this very heartfelt and personal account be commensurate with the enjoyment Charles and I have experienced in relating it to you.

Before we commence our journey down memory lane, there are a few ideas that I wish to convey to you about our dynamic duo.

Literally speaking, Mr. Jimmy and Mrs. Jessie were above the crowd as they performed on the high wire in the Mighty Haag Show. Figuratively, as they defied injury and/or death on their high wire and in their amazing, daring exploits, they were always "above the crowd" to most of the people who knew and admired them. Indeed, they were different and extraordinary!

They were a magnificent, talented, artistic, athletic, and beautiful duo waiting to present their acts of daring to the crowd below.

They were my friends from the moment I knew them. There is much about their lives I find so interesting that I have elected them as the subjects of this stroll down the avenue of loving memories.

Presenting in a manner as glorious as I can afford, is a storied account of an unforgettable couple, Mr. Jimmy and Mrs. Jessie Walters.

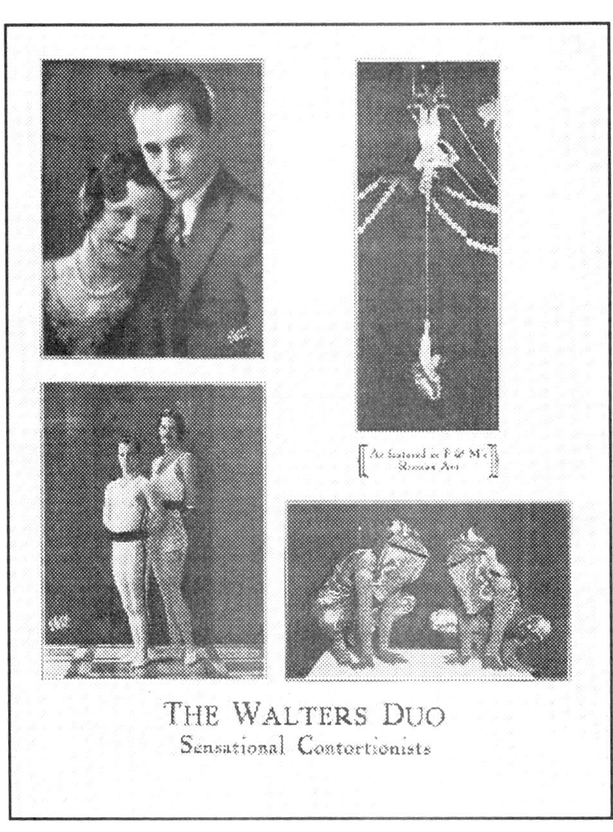

THE WALTERS DUO
Sensational Contortionists

PROLOGUE

To begin: Let me paint a picture for your imagination. The scene is an extraordinary one. It is that of a circus, the "Mighty Haag Show." Outside the tent there is mostly silence and inactivity but inside there is much ado. The tent is packed to capacity and is filled with excitement and anticipation. The crowd is rapt in the moment as two figures ascend the ladder to the high wire. Suddenly, an intrepid duo appears upon the scene and above the crowd. Immediately, the throng cheers enthusiastically in awe. They are truly agog. Suddenly the crowd's attention is transfixed upon an amazing twosome, Jimmy and Jessie Walters, as they perform exploits of daring artistry and skill without safety nets. These amazing and fearless performers are the subject of my stroll down memory lane.

As long as I can remember, I have respected, admired, and loved these people, who later became devoted and dear friends to me and my family. Because of my profound admiration and unmitigated love and due to the fact that their lives were unique, I have set about to share some of my memories of this truly amazing couple. Please indulge me as I recall unforgettable exploits of the past. It is my fervent desire that you find my recollections as interesting as I do.

CHAPTER I

Every life is a great story waiting to be told. Perhaps, this is just another of these stories; yet, upon close reflection I have decided that this story is so different from the ordinary that it implores to be expounded. My motives are pure in this endeavor. I only hope to reveal to you facts that will illuminate the character of two of the most interesting people I have ever known. These two people were known as the "Walters Duo," whose stage names were "Jessie and Jimmy Walters." (Fig. 1)

Initially, let me tell you a little about the "Mighty Haag Show." It was one of the most widely known southern circuses, starting as a wagon show in 1894, in Shreveport, Louisiana, and lasting for forty-six years. It grew steadily through 1909, when it became a railroad circus.

Ernest Haag returned it to a wagon show. The show actually opened in Marianna, Florida, on March 20, 1926. The motorized show continued in the southern territory until 1938.

In 1919, the show came to Graceville and Marianna, Florida. In 1922, Mr. Haag decided to winter the show in Marianna. It wintered in Marianna every year until 1940. Mr. Haag died on February 1, 1935, and his funeral was held at the First Presbyterian Church, Marianna, Florida. He was buried in the old cemetery in Marianna. The widow and son ran the show until 1940, when it was sold at auction. (Fig. 2)

The Mighty Haag circus parade, downtown in Marianna, Florida, was an event to which the whole town and surrounding towns looked forward. The famed Harry James played in the band, which played at the Circus Parade and the Satsuma Festival. The show was sold at auction on

September 7, 1940. There were only two places in Florida where circuses wintered: Sarasota and Marianna.*

In conversation with me, Herman Laramore, an attorney and business man in Marianna, Florida, related a very interesting story about the Haag Show. Herman owns a large expanse south of Marianna, where he has built a lovely home. He stated that just a few yards back in the woods behind his home there is a stone wall still partially standing, and the area is called "Haag Hill." This area was where the Mighty Haag Show kept all the animals used in the circus; such as elephants, lions, tigers, and monkeys, while the show wintered in Marianna.

During the time the Mighty Haag Show reposed in Marianna, the Haag family was raising their family and had quarters above the circus. Their son, Harry, was attending school at Marianna High School. He was driven to school by Guy Smuck in the clown car, "Little Austin." (I believe it was, probably, an Austin Healy.)

The Mighty Haag Show also boasted of having the only woman clown in America (possibly, Gail Boyd, who was a clown in 1925).

*(this information comes from Charles F. and Helene Wychoff, Greenwood, Florida)

Fig. 1

Fig. 2

CHAPTER II

Mr. Jimmy was born in Kentucky on November 11, 1902, to John F. James ("Pop") and Stella Klein James, as Leon K. James. (Fig. 3) Pop was employed by Standard Oil Corporation in Louisville, Kentucky as an accountant/bookkeeper. He, later, moved to New York, where he still worked with the oil corporation. (Fig. 4) Stella, his wife, whom I never knew, was born in Germany to Henry and Rebesker Klein in 1875 (according to the 1910 United States Federal Census). This family immigrated to the United States and lived in New York. I have read, at least, one article stating she was an opera singer. Stella was an attractive lady of diminutive stature. Mr. Jimmy inherited the latter trait from her. His stature in height might have been diminutive, however, his stature in accomplishments was monumental. He was approximately 4'8" tall. Stella died February 22, 1934, of uterine cancer. At this time they had moved to Tulsa, Oklahoma, and she was buried in Tulsa. Pop was still with the oil corporation, and from his earnings and investments accumulated an estate of around $75,000 in stocks and bonds.

I know little about Mr. Jimmy's early years growing up in Kentucky and New York, but by his own admission, he left home early in life. Whether he left home because he was mistreated or he was just unhappy and anxious to get on with his life, he never told us.

He was a freelance thinker from the standpoint of politics, religion, biology, and many other subjects. During his early years, he did work in a library; that tells me he was a bibliophile. Probably, he began at that time collecting some of the many books he owned. He was anxious to learn. Therefore, he probably spent lots of time reading.

He worked a little over a year in the American Museum of Natural History at 77th Street and Central Park West, New York, becoming steadily interested in probably almost every subject imaginable both arcane and ordinary. However, according to the following letter (Fig. 5) they were forced to dispense with his services. In my mind, I feel he was a self-made, self-taught genius.

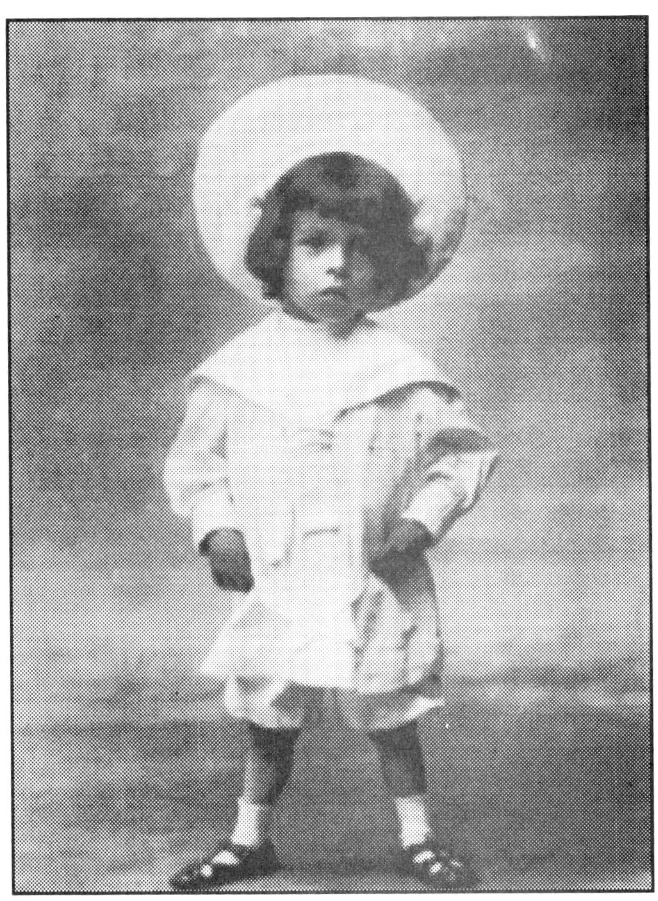

Fig. 3

Fig. 4

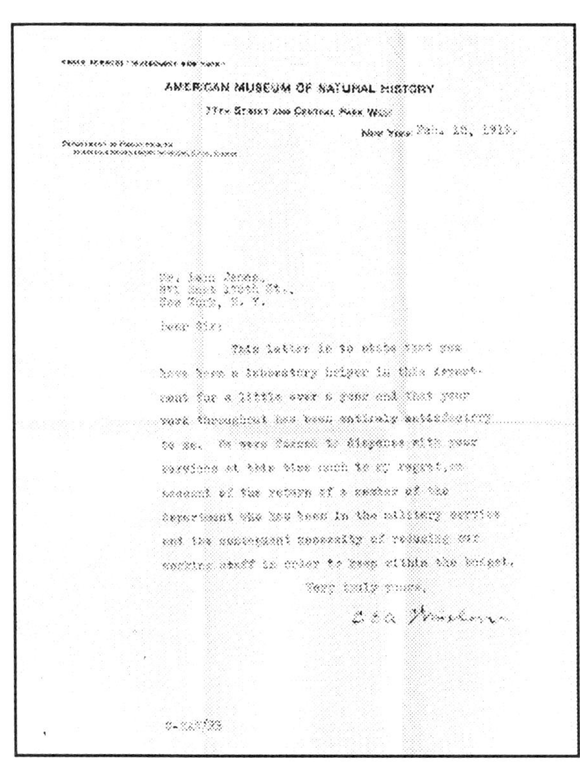

AMERICAN MUSEUM OF NATURAL HISTORY

77th Street and Central Park West

New York [illegible], 1919.

[illegible]

Dear Sir:

This letter is to state that you have been a laboratory helper in this department for a little over a year and that your work throughout has been entirely satisfactory to me. We were forced to dispense with your services at this time much to my regret, on account of the return of a member of the department who has been in the military service and the consequent necessity of reducing our working staff in order to keep within the budget.

Very truly yours,

[illegible]

Fig. 5

CHAPTER III

Although I have no understanding of his *raison d'etre*, Mr. Jimmy had a profound appreciation for life that extended beyond the realm of ordinary comprehension.

I'm sure Mr. Jimmy kept in touch with his parents in some manner; probably, it was by letter or whatever other means that might have been possible during that time. He states in his diary that he received packages from home. There is one letter available (Fig. 6), wherein he wrote his parents and sent an article (Fig. 7) asking them to keep it for him. He also identified himself to them in the article. How often he kept in touch, I do not know. At least, he did not leave home and never turn back -- he kept in touch. How and when he became affiliated with the Mighty Haag Show, I'm not sure. It must have been at an early age.

The Mighty Haag Show did winter in Marianna, Florida, sometime during the years of 1923 to 1926. By this time Mr. Jimmy was an aerialist with the show with the stage name of "James Walters," permanent address: Billboard Magazine; Cincinnati, Ohio. (Fig. 8) He was not only an aerialist with the show, he was a contortionist and known as the "Human Frog." (Fig. 9) Mr. Jimmy had agents who placed him with other shows, including the "Robinson Brothers Circus," the "Shriner's Circus," and many others. He traveled, literally, all over the United States with his act. According to his diaries, '1931-32, he traveled from New York to San Francisco. Most circuses were on the road ten months a year and traveled to as many as one hundred cities per year.

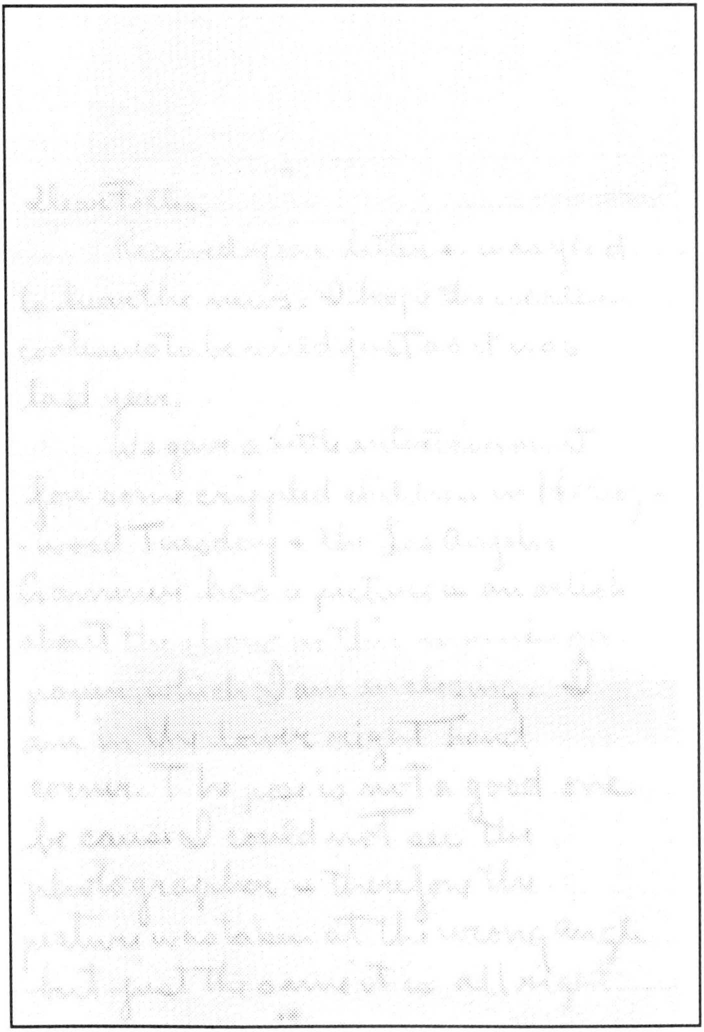

Fig. 6a

I [illegible] going to [illegible] this
article [illegible] picture for me.

The new [illegible] were to be [illegible]
[illegible] so [illegible] when they come
[illegible].

There is a large carnival right
across the street from us. The
name of it is The Great [illegible]
Shows.

Well I am continuing this
letter again here in Pomona. I held
the letter because the new [illegible]
will not be out until this afternoon.
The [illegible] just came out now
as I am writing this letter, which
runs up to Nov. 12. I guess Nano
will be on the next [illegible] card.

Will close now [illegible]

[illegible]

Leon

Fig. 6b

Children at Hospital Thrilled by Big Circus

By Lannie Haynes Martin

[illegible]

Fig. 7a

Fig. 7b

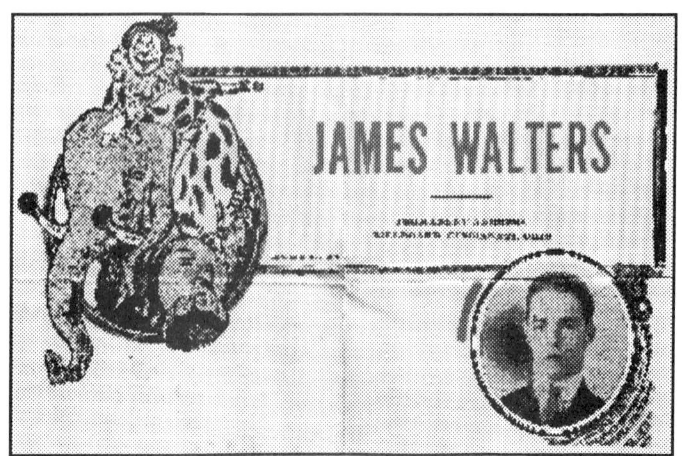

Fig. 8

Fig. 9

CHAPTER IV

During the time of the show wintering in Marianna, Mr. Jimmy lived at the Chipola Hotel, which was built in 1883, and which at the time was only a two story wooden building with twenty-five rooms. It had comfortable rooms, wash basins, mosquito netting around the beds, and slop jars (earlier term for bedpan). (Fig. 10)

The hotel was purchased by J. C. Corcoran. It was moved to the back of the existing lot, and when completed, it was a five story building with seventy-five rooms.(Fig.11) The hotel hosted approximately one-hundred cast members from the Haag Show while they wintered in Marianna.

Mr. Jimmy always dined in a little restaurant or cafe located very near the hotel. While dining in one of these small cafes, he met a tall, thin, lovely young female who was working as a waitress. This young lady was Mrs. Jessie. Mrs. Jessie was from the Lovedale-Two Egg community and was trying to make a living for herself and her small child. She had married William Pyke at an early age. Her husband was born in 1887, and died at an early age in August of 1922. There was a son born during this union. His name was W. H. Pyke, Jr., who was born September 9, 1919.

Fig. 10

Fig. 11

CHAPTER V

I have spent much time in the recollection of Mr. Jimmy. After all, he was the progenitor of the "Walters Duo." Surely, Mr. Jimmy is the subject of many of the anecdotes that I have chosen to convey to you. (Fig.12)

Regardless of my attention to Mr. Jimmy, I have much to assert about his beloved spouse, Mrs. Jessie. There is voluminous information about Mrs. Jessie that I have failed to relate in this missive of love.

In her own right, Mrs. Jessie was an interesting and extraordinary person. Consider this: She was a very lonely person in a rural area without any visible means of extricating herself from the mundane life that enveloped her. Perhaps, she was depressed on that day in Marianna, when she first met Mr. Jimmy. Maybe, because she was lonely and downtrodden, the introduction of Mr. Jimmy into her life was a joy beyond imagination. He wooed and mesmerized her into a state of complete submission. (Fig. 13)

Yielding to her lower instincts as many people are disposed to do, Mrs. Jessie forsook all of her parental responsibilities, cast off her normal duties of life to the winds of irresponsibility, and dedicated her life to the world of show business with her newly found saviour, Mr. Jimmy.

Yes, Mr. Jimmy was an amazing person, who had rescued her from an extremely boring life.

In making the decision, Mrs. Jessie was freed from the ennui of her previous life; but she was to become, forever, shackled with the guilt of knowing that in pursuing her dream, she had deserted her only heir, her dear son, W. H. What a price it was to follow a dream while forsaking the welfare and love of an only offspring.

Whether it was right or wrong, who can say? Mrs. Jessie, I am sure, faced the dilemma of answering this query the rest of her life. But like the rest of humanity, she made a decision that had to bear its own consequences. Whether the sacrifice she made was worth the acclaim she experienced in show business will never be known.

Mr. Jimmy was very involved with his livelihood; and being an aerialist and having his own act, the most important thing in his life, at that time, was "The show must go on." When he met Mrs. Jessie, a tall, lovely, thin, young lady, working as a waitress, he could imagine how nice it would be to have a wife and how his act could be much improved with a partner. I'm not saying he did not love her, but that he could see a future with her. I'll always believe he loved her dearly.

Fig. 12

Fig. 13

CHAPTER VI

Mrs. Jessie left her son with his father's mother, Rhoda Elizabeth Pyke, whose husband, W. H. Pyke, had died in 1915. She lived in the Lovedale-Two Egg community. He lived with his Granny Pyke until her death in October, 1929. At that time, with his trunk of toys sent to him by his mother, he moved to his Aunt Annie Pyke Ford's home. Aunt Annie had four daughters: Inez, Mary Lizzie, Maude, and Annie Ross. He seemed to be much happier, because he had children with whom he could play. I believe he also visited and lived, at times, with other aunts in the community, Mrs. Lucy Pyke and Mrs. Laura Bazzell. (Fig. 14)

Aunt Annie Pyke Ford and Rhoda Elizabeth and husband, W. H. Pyke, were charter members of the Lovedale Baptist Church established in 1899.

Fig. 14

CHAPTER VII

Soon after their marriage on March 7, 1923, Mr. Jimmy and Mrs. Jessie left Marianna with the show and traveled all over the United States. During this time Mr. Jimmy taught Mrs. Jessie the art of aerialism and contortionism. (Fig. 15 thru 18)

According to his diary, Mr. Jimmy, on February 17, 1931, bought Mrs. Jessie a wedding ring and they were married again on February 19, 1931, possibly, in the name of Leon K. James.

There is a possibility that he married Mrs. Jessie another time or two, I'm just not certain about this.

Of this I am certain: After Mrs. Jessie's death, he wanted to marry her again; however, he could not find anyone willing to perform the ceremony. Finally, a Justice of the Peace agreed to marry him again to Mrs. Jessie, if he would have someone stand in for Mrs. Jessie. He came to my mother and asked her if she would do this. With much reluctance, but with respect for Mr. Jimmy, she did so.

The fact that Mr. Jimmy married Mrs. Jessie so many times may appear as bizarre behavior. But remember this, Mr. Jimmy was an eccentric man and, perhaps, because of his extreme intelligence and perception was a man of many idiosyncrasies, which are often, but not necessarily, attended by genius.

Fig. 15

Fig. 16

Fig. 17

THE WALTERS DUO
Presenting their original sensational spin
from the rigging to the ground, attaining
a speed of over 500 revolutions a minute

Fig. 18

CHAPTER VIII

Mrs. Jessie was always mesmerized in a way with Mr. Jimmy. She was, also, fascinated with his knowledge and his attitude and affection toward her. Mrs. Jessie was rather timid in the beginning, meek and very soft spoken. It was always evident that Mr. Jimmy was the bold one in the family and Mrs. Jessie always accepted his domination. In my presence, I never heard either one of them say harsh words to each other, although there were times when I felt she was intimidated by Mr. Jimmy.

He was, in a way, domineering; and Mrs. Jessie always gave in to his demands. I believe Mrs. Jessie was deeply in love with Mr. Jimmy and felt indebted to him for having given her the opportunity to travel the nation. Otherwise, she might have been a Two Egg girl or a waitress the remainder of her life!

At this point, I'd like to just give you some examples of how they lived while on the road traveling from city to city performing their act. These come from his diary of 1931.

> On January 3, 1931, they received a letter telling them to be ready to leave soon. They practiced their act each. day with the uprights at home before they left.
>
> On January 10, 1931, they left for Chicago, Illinois, by train from Cowarts, Alabama, and arrived January 11th on the "Dixie Limited." They visited the new Aquarium and Field Museum. It was nothing to compare with the New York Aquarium. The Field Museum is both a natural history and art museum combined. They attended a movie, and saw "Soldiers' Play Thing," by Vina Delmar.
>
> On January 13th they left on a trip to Los Angeles and arrived on January 16th. The Shriner's Circus

opened on the 17th. They did their act in the afternoon and at night on the 17th through the 20th. They were taken by friends out to Hollywood and Beverly Hills, and the friends pointed out all the interesting places. They also did their "Frog Act" for the children at the Shriner's Hospital at this time. They received their contracts for Minneapolis and St. Paul. They continued their act on the 21st through the 25th. They signed their contracts with Fanchon and Marco to work "in production." They saw and heard Admiral Byrd speak at the auditorium. They left for Chicago on the 27th and arrived on January 30th.

This is just one month of their travels. Can you imagine a young lady from Two Egg being able to travel and experience such travels?

They traveled the cities of New York, Philadelphia, Chicago, Minneapolis, Los Angeles, San Diego, Hollywood, Portland, Seattle, Denver, St. Louis, Detroit, Milwaukee, Beverly Hills, St. Paul, Pasadena, Fresno, San Jose, San Francisco, Oakland, Tacoma, Niagara Falls, and saw many of the interesting points in each city.

The following is an excerpt from Mr. Jimmy's diary for the next five months of the Walters Duo:

February, 1931
<u>Chicago</u>

While in Chicago they located a light house keeping room with a kitchenette. They saw several movies. He ordered a brown suit from Nash Co. paying only $20.60 for it. They visited with a lot of the "bunch" in "The Magic Carpet."

Received letter from Roy Beall from Malone, Florida, offering spring oats for the farm at 87½ cents per bushel; by wire ordered eight bushels for $7.00.

They visited the Lincoln Park Zoo, "very nice." "Saw the smallest baby elephant ever." Letter from Fanchon and Marco saying they will open March 19th. Bought book, "Navigating the Air." Friends came over and we enjoyed the visit. Lincoln's birthday; went to the Curtises, had dinner and spent pleasant afternoon and evening.

Went to Art Institute and Public Library, Jessie stayed home. Bought book; "Aero planes Past, Present, Future," by Graham White, used $2.00.

Saw movie starring Richard Dix. Leaving tonight, February 21st for

Minneapolis:

February 23 thru 28 did acts at least two, three or four per day with Shriner's Circus; did double aerial contortion, featuring revolve, did Double Frog contortion. On February 26 went to Shriner's Hospital in A.M. and did Frog Act for kiddies. (Fig. 19) Shriners put on swell affair for the people with the show at the Raddison. Jessie bought a pretty red dress here. March 1, 1931:

St. Paul:

Saw "Lucky Boys" at the R.K.O. house, swell act.

March 2nd, opened with Shriner Circus, two acts per day through March 6th. Three shows on the 7th. Left on 11:00 o'clock train, lost glasses. March 8th and 9th en route to

Los Angeles:

Arriving in Los Angeles at 5:45, stopping at the Cecil. March 11th through 17th visited Fanchon and Marco. March 18th had showing of "Russian Art." at the Manchester; one show at night. Found glasses in rigging box.

Pasadena:

March 19th opened at the Colorado and showed two and three shows per day through March 25th. Back to

Los Angeles:

At the Lowe's State on March 26th. Saw Ricardo Ashforth at R.K.O. Four shows per night through April 1st and one Midnight show.

San Diego:

April 2nd through 8th Fox Theater; four shows per day. Saw preview of the picture "Skippy," a great picture.

Hollywood:

April 9th through 15th. Pantages Theater, three to four shows per day. Bought several books, and stayed in

Hollywood for the next week. While there went to Los Angeles bought some old aviation magazines at the Los Angeles Library. Saw "Hells Angels".

Fresno:

April 22nd, en route

April 23rd through 25th Fox-Wilmont Theater, three to four shows per day.

San Francisco:

April 30th through May 6th, Warfield Theater. Saw Miss Allen who used to be "Prima Dona" on Robinson Show in 1927. Showed three to four times per day.

Oakland:

May 7th through 13th, Fox-Oakland Theater, four shows per day and one midnight show.

Portland:

En Route on May 14th.
May 15th through 20th, Paramount Theater, four shows each day and one midnight show.

Seattle:

May 21st through 27th, Paramount Theater, four shows each day.

Tacoma:

May 28th, visited friends and went to see Al G. Barnes Show, free passes.

May 29th through 31st, Broadway Theater, four shows per day.

Denver:

En route on June 1st and 2nd.

June 3rd through 6th, Denver Theater, four shows each day.

June 7th, Sunday, had a wonderful trip up Lookout Mountains, saw Buffalo Bill's and his wife's graves, also Buffalo Bill Museum. Drove 88 miles in all.

June 8th and 9th, Denver Theater, four shows per day.

June 10th en route to St. Louis:

June 11th and 12th Fox Theater, four shows each day. "This has been rather an eventful day for me-received an answer to my letter from Harold who sent me three very interesting Post Cards that he bought in France-they picture three early type aero planes- Odeir-Vendome, De Pischoff & De Lesseps, Bleuit monoplane.

Also received a letter from an artist, Robert Bushnell Hyman of 520 Madison Ave., New York, who is making a collection of contortionists pictures, and wants one of ours. He enclosed check for one dollar which I am going to return. Also, enjoyed a pleasant hour at the public library here.

St. Louis:

June 13th, Fox Theater, four shows, Looked through a telescope on a street corner and viewed Saturn and the stars Vega and Arcturus, according to the man operating the telescope. June 14th, Fox Theater, four shows. Went to Forest Park Zoo in the morning, enjoyed few hours I had very much, especially enjoyed the reptile exhibits. June 15th, Fox Theater, four shows. Jessie doing scissors for finale in place of spin because my left eye was bloodshot from high altitude in Denver. June 16th, Fox Theater, four shows, Jessie still doing scissors, my eye getting along nicely. Went to see the Lindberg Collection of trophies at the Jefferson Memorial. Then, went over to the zoo to see the Bird House and the Elephant Seal of which they had two living specimens.

June 7th, Fox Theater, four shows, Jessie still doing scissor dislocations for finale. We saw Shaw's Gardens this morning and had enjoyable trip through the grounds and conservatories.

Milwaukee:

June 18th through 24th, four shows. Went to museum here and enjoyed the few hours there, especially the Entomological Exhibits. Jessie still doing finale. Went to doctor, eye doing nicely, will be able to revolve in a few days. Also, went to public museum on two different occasions.

June 25th, en route to

Detroit:

June 26th through July 2nd, Fox Theater, four shows per day, Jessie still doing finale, eye getting along fine. (Fig. 20)

Niagara Falls:

July 3rd through 9th, three to four shows per
day at Strand Theater.

July 6th "Had a most enjoyable day, got up early, had breakfast then we walked over to Goat Island and went to see the "Cave of the Winds," a really thrilling experience." Then we went to see the "Maid of the Mist" on the little boat that goes right up to the Falls and turns around right by the "Horseshoe Falls." While this was a nice trip we both enjoyed the "Cave of the Winds" the best, and then after the show at night we walked over the bridge to the Canadian side to view the Falls that are truly beautiful as they are played upon with the many colored search lights, and as the colors are skillfully blended from one shade to another. Between shows, I went to the museum here which is privately owned and has a 50 cents admission charge. They have an exhibit, two barrels and an iron tank that have carried people over the Falls, and down "Whirlpool Rapids."

Again, let us endeavor to perceive how Mrs. Jessie must have felt when she was able to see all these sights for the first time and how amazed she must have been!

Fig. 19

MOTION PICTURE
ATTRACTIONS
Biggest Show in Detroit
25¢ TO 1 P.M.
50¢ FROM 1 P.M.
FOX
'ANNABELLE'S
AFFAIRS'
Victor McLaglen
Jeanette MacDonald
Roland Young
Stage
Russian Art IDEA
Featuring
BILL TELAAK
with BUD HANLEY
STAN
MEYERS
MIDNIGHT SHOW
TONITE 11:45

Fig. 20

CHAPTER IX

In the following revelations about Mrs. Jessie's life, I hope to reveal some kind of insight about this wonderful, amazing person and how she became the heroine who, eventually, inspired me in this literary endeavor. What she became is a matter of record; what she felt, one can only surmise.

In a circumspect manner, I have approached the subject. Only providence can grant me the wisdom to appraise and objectify the information at my disposal into a comprehensive true nature, or character. Please indulge me as I travel from what actually occurred in the past to what may have transpired to make it so.

Imagine this:

> It was the beginning of an exciting night at the Mighty Haag Show. Mrs. Jessie was in her dressing room waiting to put the finishing touches on her costume and makeup before emerging to the excited crowd outside. She started to exit the tent when she glimpsed her reflection in the mirror that hung near the exit. Suddenly, she was compelled to gaze at the image before her. Who was that person that stared at her from the mirror?
>
> Ready to make her entrance outside and to ascend the high wire, she was rapt in wonderment and pondered who she really was. Was she the lonely woebegone person who not so long ago had watched the nights go by in lonely reverie? No, she was a famous member of the magnificent Walters Duo, an acclaimed performer of the Mighty Haag

Show. She, at last, was somebody; indeed she was a star! She thought to herself, "I should be happy, so why am I not?"

As the band played triumphantly awaiting her entrance, she paused and mused upon her life.

Was reaching stardom on the high wire of the Mighty Haag Show worth the sacrifices she had made on her journey to fame?

She had a son, W. H., whom she dearly loved. Was forsaking him at an early age worth the adoration of a mesmerizing stranger she had met in Marianna and the life of fame and excitement that ensued? The answer to the foregoing questions may never be known.

Indeed, in many ways Mrs. Jessie's life was a dramatic one. However, let us deal with some of the more mundane aspects of her being.

In a conversation with Nancy Macklin, granddaughter of Will Keith and niece of Mrs. Jessie, I learned the following information: Mrs. Jessie was born to Andrew J. Keith and Martha Hawthorne Keith, who died while in Texas and was buried there. However, Andrew was buried at the Methodist Church cemetery in Bascom, Florida. According to Nancy the Keiths had come to Bascom from Texas.

Mrs. Jessie had four sisters: Edell, Ruth, Minnie, and Beulah. She also had three brothers: Will, John, and Robert. To the best of my knowledge all of the sisters and brothers are now deceased. However, there is one brother, John, about whose fate I am not sure. He left home early in life and never returned. We can only speculate that he is now deceased.

I knew, personally, Edell, who at one time was married to a Coleman. Ruth and Harry Bender were married and both at one time worked with the Haag Show. I do, vaguely, remember Minnie and Beulah.

Remarkably, I also recall Will, who lived in the Bascom area. He married Cora Johnson and they had several children: James, Evelyn, Louise, Reuben, Willie Pearl, Douglas, and Junior. All are deceased except Junior; and he is in his eighties.

In supplying all of this information about Mrs. Jessie's family I hope I have not lulled you into a somnolent state. Notwithstanding this possibility, I felt it necessary to convey this information for the few people who might be interested.

CHAPTER X

Mr. Jimmy and Mrs. Jessie came home regularly to visit her son and, eventually, retired in the Neal's Landing-Mt. Olive community near Bascom, Florida. He built their home on the acreage he had purchased during the years (the acreage was approximately one hundred eighty acres). They had one of the only houses in this area that had a bathroom and running water. And, if I remember correctly, they had the only windmill in this area.

In the home was the nicest and largest library I'd ever seen. Indeed, it was the only one I'd ever been in! My brother, sister, and I were allowed to enter the library and enjoy viewing the many books. Sometimes, Mr. Jimmy and Mrs. Jessie would talk to us about some of the books and they told us many stories about their travels. However, we were taught very early, by our parents, "Do Not Touch," and of course, we did not. Because of this, we were some of the few children allowed in the library.

At this time, after having purchased the acreage, Mr. Jimmy had to learn all about farming. He was a city boy, grew up in New York and knew nothing about farming. He built a tenant house on the property and hired families at different times to live and farm for him. Like sharecroppers with an experienced farmer, he could learn by actually watching and working along with the farmer. He made notes and read books about when to buy seed, when to plant, and how to plow. He also learned to clear some of the land to have more room to plant and raise livestock.

At one time or other he had Carlos and Catherine Wilkinson occupy the tenant house. He learned from Carlos many usual, as well as unusual, things about the art of farming. At one time he had Harmon and Mrs. Mary Strickland occupy the tenant house; and he surely was taught many things by them. However, in the meantime, he studied and read books to know more about the cultivation of plants. He planted corn, peanuts, cotton, and the land builders necessary to keep the land up to par.

CHAPTER XI

Let us pause here to reflect upon my motives in this exposition of two people who have given me so many happy memories. I hope my revelations do not make Mr. Jimmy and Mrs. Jessie appear as Godlike individuals without fault. Indeed, there is no human being above imperfection. Mr. Jimmy and Mrs. Jessie were no exceptions. Let me reiterate an example.

I think, probably, the worst time in their lives was after W. H. went away to serve in the United States Army Air Force for many years and returned. He had changed so much. He now was using alcoholic beverages and smoking -- deleterious habits which had never been tolerated in their home. On many occasions W. H. mistreated both Mr. Jimmy and Mrs. Jessie. Sometime, I believe, he resented the fact that Mrs. Jessie made her decision to be with Mr. Jimmy and left him behind. And when he began to drink, these feelings of resentment were more pronounced in his mind and he spoke many harsh and curse words toward Mrs. Jessie on many different occasions. I don't believe W. H. ever injured his mother physically, but mentally he wounded her deeply. I'm sure Mr. Jimmy and Mrs. Jessie had harsh discussions about the situation between them and W. H. I was told that on one occasion when W. H. was drinking, he came to the museum and spit in Mrs. Jessie's face. After that altercation, I don't believe Mrs. Jessie ever saw W. H. again before her death.

W. H. went on about his life, remarried, had a child and lived as normally as possible. I'm not sure whether the child was permitted to visit Mrs. Jessie. In fact, I'm not sure the child was born before Mrs. Jessie's death. (Fig. 21)

Let me say they had their ups and downs, bad times and good times. They were not perfect by a long shot. They had their faults as do we all.

After Mr. Jimmy and Mrs. Jessie retired and returned to this area, they still loved to go to good movies. During their travels across the United States they attended many movies and met many stars. They were good friends with Tom Mix (Fig.22), and they met Marlene Dietrich. The nearest movies in this area were located in Donalsonville, Georgia.

Fig. 21

OFFICIAL ROUTE
SEASON 1930
SELLS FLOTO CIRCUS
FEATURING
TOM MIX AND TONY
THE WONDER HORSE
PERMANENT ADDRESS
PERU, INDIANA

Fig. 22

CHAPTER XII

There is one person that in this walk through the vale of memories is pronouncedly unforgettable, Charles King. Mr. Jimmy was so significant in his bearing upon the lives of many persons. One of these individuals was Charles. When Mr. Jimmy entered his life, Charles was young and filled with wonder, amazement, and curiosity, and often contemplated the myriad facets of an ever evolving universe. Maybe his life and mind would never have been piqued to the great intensity it realized were it not for the arrival into his life of such an extraordinary, cogent, mental giant. Mr. Jimmy and Charles spent many hours together discussing numerous subjects, some esoteric and others ordinary but more profound than most individuals ever experience. Charles was eager and excited to learn and Mr. Jimmy afforded him so many diverse avenues into the world of knowledge.

Charles recalls many incidents regarding his association with Mr. Jimmy. He and his sisters, Lillian and Louise, loved the movies. They had no way to go to Donalsonville, Georgia, where the movies were being shown. Mr. Jimmy and Mrs. Jessie were like "angels of mercy" to them. They would come by and take them to the movies. Charles really loved the movies; probably, no one was as enraptured by the "flickering of celluloid" as he. Actually, his jaunts to the movies proved to be a revelation and a blessing. Charles always wanted to sit on the front row. Due to the astute observation of Mr. Jimmy and Mrs. Jessie, Charles' parents were encouraged to have his eyes examined by an optometrist. They did so, and to this day Charles wears corrective lenses. Charles is eternally grateful. Because of the caring actions of two wonderful people, he was afforded the sight he had never before known. To this day he is always thankful that he was a guest of two exceptional individuals on a splendid night at the movies.

Trips to Donalsonville were special to Charles. He related to me one incident involving a trip to the movies. Before proceeding to the theater for the movies, Mr. Jimmy and Mrs. Jessie took Charles and Lillian by the Piggly Wiggly store, located on the main street of Donalsonville. The floor was wooden and Charles was barefoot -- an accident waiting to happen. (May I say that going barefoot was not uncommon in the area at this time.) Suddenly, Charles gasped in pain as a splinter from the floor pierced the sole of his foot. Mr. Jimmy and Mrs. Jessie, always the care-givers, immediately took him to the nearby hospital, where Dr. Mosely removed the splinter. Charles was somewhat taken aback by the remarks of the curmudgeonly physician who sarcastically replied, "Next time break your neck." Charles was not amused.

There are many events that Charles recalls about his association with Mr. Jimmy and Mrs. Jessie. In addition to his many scientific and religious topics of discussion with Mr. Jimmy, Charles would at times take the dictionary and randomly pick any word, and to his consternation Mr. Jimmy never failed to define the word in an accurate and concise manner.

CHAPTER XIII

In the following revelation there is no amusement or even peace unless you have a proclivity for the cruel and the bizarre. Indeed, it is a setting for a horror story waiting to be told.

Imagine this: A person is taken and deprived of all outside activity and experiences and compelled to drink liquor in order to coerce him to sign checks of varying denominations. He is not given the opportunity to make any outside contacts. Every time he begs for mercy his pleas are stifled by more alcohol; he is completely inebriated and beyond conscious or sensible actions. This is a setting for a heinous story waiting to be proclaimed. Such is the story of Pop.

Pop, Mr. Jimmy's father, was a wealthy man who had lived most of his life in the New York City area. He worked as an auditor/bookkeeper with the Standard Oil Corporation, beginning in Louisville, Kentucky, New York, New York, and finally in Tulsa, Oklahoma. His wife died in February, 1934, in Tulsa. Subsequently, Mr. Jimmy and Mrs. Jessie traveled to Tulsa and brought Pop from Tulsa down to Mr. Jimmy's home to retire and live with Mr. Jimmy and Mrs. Jessie. He, at that time or soon afterwards, was the owner of a private airplane. It was a 1938 Aeronca Model KCA. Whether he was a pilot himself, I do not know.

While living with Mr. Jimmy and Mrs. Jessie, Pop would often go into Marianna, spend the night at the Chipola Hotel and visit some of the places that were not so desirable.

Because of his addiction to alcohol and hedonistic lifestyle, Pop was not the easiest person with whom to associate. Notwithstanding his faults, Pop did have a good and lovable side. During his sober and lucid moments, he was charming and, somewhat, beguiling to the many friends who loved and appreciated him. (Fig.23) Among the many people who loved him, in spite of his "Mr. Hyde" persona while under the influence of alcohol, was his son, Mr. Jimmy.

Although, Pop was at times one of the most difficult persons imaginable, Mr. Jimmy deeply loved him. He did everything humanly possible to assure the care and welfare of his dear Pop. Only God can know the sorrow and pain that Mr. Jimmy suffered while his beloved father was incarcerated in the Florida State Hospital in Chattahoochee, Florida.

Pop sometimes drank too much and would stay away from home for several days or weeks. During this time he hired Tommy Saliba as his personal pilot. Many of the local people might still remember Tommy and Tee Saliba. It is rumored that at one time they ran a bar, grill, or restaurant in the basement of the Chipola Hotel. Perhaps, this is unsubstantiated hearsay; Saliba did, at one time, operate the Splendid Cafe, which was located on Constitution Lane along about where Marianna Office Supply is located at the present time. Tee Saliba, his wife, operated Tee's Grill, located across the street from the Post Office, where Hinson Insurance is presently located. Tee later was known as Tee Hodges. She continued to operate Tee's Grill in the same location. She was later known as Tee Heald and ran The Caravan, located at Highway 71 and Highway 90.

One day after Pop had been away from home for several weeks, Mr. Jimmy received a letter from a maid working for the Salibas, telling Mr. Jimmy that Pop was locked inside the house and that he should try to see about him. Many efforts by Mr. Jimmy, by Mrs. Jessie, and by Mrs. Jessie's son were made to see Pop. However all efforts were in vain.

The Salibas would not permit them to see Pop. After all efforts were exhausted and Mr. Jimmy knew of no other recourse, he pursued a court order to get Pop out of the house. The court order was granted.

Fig. 23

CHAPTER XIV

What caused Pop to succumb to the immoral overtures of two callous, manipulative, money-grubbing scoundrels like Tee and Tommy Saliba? Ostensibly, he was confused or maybe just a lonely old man starving for attention and seeking affection in all the wrong places. Whatever the reason for his indiscretions, none were worthy of the vile acts perpetrated upon him by two persons who were, in all probability, considered of good repute by their associates and friends. Greed is perhaps one of the greatest sins in which mankind immerses itself and wallows in self-indulgent delight. The Salibas exemplified this heinous behavior with impunity and without noticeable remorse.

On or about June of 1937, Pop left the Chipola Hotel and went to live with the Salibas at the insistence of Tee Saliba. He lived with the Salibas until October of 1938 when he was adjudged insane. He was locked inside the Saliba home in July, 1938, and was incarcerated there by the Salibas, until October, 1938.

During the period from June, 1937, to October, 1938, he signed 177 checks to Cash for amounts ranging from a few dollars to $15,000, totaling $27,100, which were cashed for the Salibas benefit or deposited in their account by the Salibas. The $15,000 check was dated September 8, 1938. In January, 1938, the house of the Salibas burned and he gave them a check for $3,000 to rebuild, noting, however, on his check stub that this $3,000 was a loan. He never made any effort to secure the same.

Prior to June 25, 1938, he signed a transfer of title to a Buick automobile he had bought to Tee Saliba. He signed a Last Will and Testament purporting to make Tom Saliba his sole beneficiary.

Pop also paid for a steno course taken in Dothan, Alabama, by Ruby Hill, niece of the Salibas. It was thought that she had typed or prepared the Will dated August 4, 1938. Pop's signature was witnessed by Paul McIntyre, driver for Nehi Bottling Company, and Rex Padgett, driver for Cheroot Bottling Company, neither of whom saw Pop sign.

Pop could never be described as chaste or beyond reproach. Perhaps, he led a life not entirely incorrupt; nonetheless he deserved to be treated with the dignity and respect afforded any human being. For this reason, I applaud him for his previous works of humanity and goodness, and furthermore, I denounce the cruel misadventures suffered by Pop at the hands of the Salibas.

At the outset, I am not absolutely positive of the events that transpired during the incarceration of Pop by the Salibas. I can only conjecture upon the probability of what might have happened. I do not know that the incidents given were entirely accurate. I only remember what Mrs. Jessie and Mr. Jimmy told me about these happenings. I do know for a fact that the matters revealed in the lawsuit by Mr. Jimmy against the Salibas are a legal fact. But has the absolute truth been unfolded here? Who can say?

Actually, in any of the amazing events that transpire in nature, there is no absolute truth. Truth is actually a concept altered by the different perceptions of many different people. This is not to say that I doubt the veracity of the foregoing observations regarding Mr. Jimmy and Mrs. Jessie. In my, perhaps, prejudiced opinion, I accept all the facts presented in the court against the Salibas. Why am I sure about the decisions provided by the court? Without hesitation, I proclaim: The evident wrong doings of the situation and the devious, immoral character of the Salibas declare it so. Unfortunately, Pop was so undernourished, weak, starved, emaciated and gaunt, and confused that he hardly knew who he was or where he was; and so, he had to be hospitalized. Eventually, he was declared incompetent, or insane, and was served with the Insanity Writ on October 20, 1938 then transported to the Florida State Hospital in Chattahoochee, Florida.

The fact is Pop died on October 21, 1948, after ten years in the hospital. Mr. Jimmy took his body by train to Tulsa, Oklahoma, to be laid to rest by his wife, Stella Klein James.

CHAPTER XV

In the beginning, approximately 1934 my mother and father, Charlie and Johnnie Bell, (Fig. 24) became good friends with Mr. Jimmy and Mrs. Jessie; how exactly I'm not quite sure. I do know that both families loved to play cards (Set Back) and board games. They even taught the three children in my family Charles, Elaine, and me how to play Set Back. Mr. Jimmy and Mrs. Jessie were very good to us as children. (Fig. 25) They always made sure that we had at least one nice gift at Christmas and they always told us such fascinating stories of their travels. When my sister Elaine was born, Mr. Jimmy's father, John F. James (Pop) named her. He gave her that beautiful name, "Elaine." We always called him "Pop" because that is what Mr. Jimmy and Mrs. Jessie called him.

Many times I remember Mr. Jimmy and Mrs. Jessie bringing Pop from the hospital out to their home for visits. My family would also visit with him. He always asked our names. When Elaine told him her name, he would always say, "That's my favorite name." But he did not remember that he named her.

Fig. 24

Fig. 25

CHAPTER XVI

In late 1938, the lawsuit entitled, "Leon K. James, as Guardian of the Estate of John F. James, an insane person, Plaintiff, vs. Tom Saliba and his wife, Tee Saliba, et al, Defendants" was filed with the Clerk of the Court of Jackson County, Florida.

Briefly, I will tell you the Court, presided over by Judge E. C. Welch, ruled in favor of Mr. Jimmy and ordered the sum of $18,321.03 seized from the bank accounts of Tom and Tee Saliba and currently held in Receivership to be returned to Pop's estate as well as the Buick automobile and the diamond rings. The dining room furniture, the china and dining room cabinet, the airplane (Fig. 26) and the brick house located in the triangle on two and one-half acres were impressed in a trust in favor of the estate at the rate of 8%. Tom and Tee Saliba were allowed ten days to purchase the same. The Last Will and Testament dated August 4, 1938, was declared null and void, cancelled and revoked. If the impressed items were not paid, with interest, within 10 days, they were to be sold. Additionally, the Salibas were ordered to pay Mr. Jimmy's legal fees in the amount of $7,500.00. The Salibas filed an appeal with the Florida Supreme Court concerning the fees. The mandate was issued July 8, 1940, affirming the decision of the lower court but reduced the legal fees from $7,500.00 to $5,000.00. All assets from the law suit available to Mr. Jimmy were given to the Salvation Army by Mr. Jimmy.

On the surface most people would surmise that the Saliba's association with Pop was convivial and kind. In all probability, it was in the beginning. Unfortunately, and without reason and unbeknownst to anyone else, the Salibas' prolonged association with Pop developed into a relationship of avarice, which sequed into malice aforethought. What a tragedy! With a human weakness for covetous abandon, they became a curse to Pop in this pathetic reckoning.

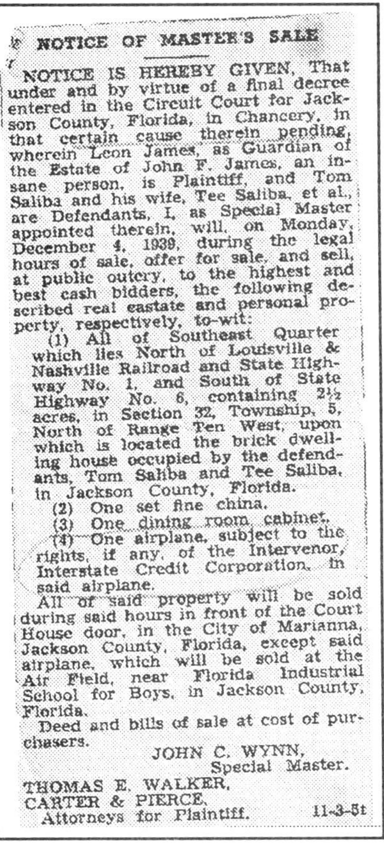

NOTICE OF MASTER'S SALE

NOTICE IS HEREBY GIVEN, That under and by virtue of a final decree entered in the Circuit Court for Jackson County, Florida, in Chancery, in that certain cause therein pending, wherein Leon James, as Guardian of the Estate of John F. James, an insane person, is Plaintiff, and Tom Saliba and his wife, Tee Saliba, et al., are Defendants, I, as Special Master appointed therein, will, on Monday, December 4, 1939, during the legal hours of sale, offer for sale, and sell, at public outcry, to the highest and best cash bidders, the following described real eastate and personal property, respectively, to-wit:

(1) All of Southeast Quarter which lies North of Louisville & Nashville Railroad and State Highway No. 1, and South of State Highway No. 6, containing 2½ acres, in Section 32, Township, 5, North of Range Ten West, upon which is located the brick dwelling house occupied by the defendants, Tom Saliba and Tee Saliba, in Jackson County, Florida.

(2) One set fine china.

(3) One dining room cabinet.

(4) One airplane, subject to the rights, if any, of the Intervenor, Interstate Credit Corporation, in said airplane.

All of said property will be sold during said hours in front of the Court House door, in the City of Marianna, Jackson County, Florida, except said airplane, which will be sold at the Air Field, near Florida Industrial School for Boys, in Jackson County, Florida.

Deed and bills of sale at cost of purchasers.

JOHN C. WYNN,
Special Master.

THOMAS E. WALKER,
CARTER & PIERCE,
Attorneys for Plaintiff. 11-3-5t

Fig. 26

CHAPTER XVII

Let's go back again to the recollection of Charles King. Previously, I have alluded to his rapport with Mr. Jimmy and Mrs. Jessie, whom he appreciated and enjoyed as friends. Charles was the son of Christian parents, J. D. and Clarice King. Mr. Jimmy and Mr. King often enjoyed discussing politics and religion. Of course, Mr. Jimmy was a professed agnostic. He was not an unbeliever in the sense that God does not exist, only that His existence cannot be proven. Really, the line between an atheist and an agnostic is very thin and the difference is, for the most part, indiscernible.

As I stated, previously, Mr. Jimmy was not an atheist; but he was certainly not a Christian. He thought religion was a creation of mankind and that the origins of the universe, the reasons for our existence, and life itself were totally and eternally inexplicable. (May I say, parenthetically, that the foregoing postulations regarding Mr. Jimmy's beliefs are fictitious and completely imaginary, but they are indeed in accordance with the reality based upon Charles' memories of him and his conversations with him.)

The Kings, although believers in Christ and His teachings, were never zealots or bigots. They loved Mr. Jimmy and Mrs. Jessie as they loved all of their fellow human beings. Indeed, they embraced and welcomed their association with them.

To this day Charles recalls, with great admiration and love, his happy association with Mr. Jimmy and Mrs. Jessie.

CHAPTER XVIII

Back during this time there was a depression in this country and our family was poor, although we, as children, did not know it. Daddy farmed a small acreage and grew our vegetables. We had cows and hogs and chickens which served as our meats; but we knew nothing about fancy or store-bought foods. I remember we visited Mrs. Jessie and Mr. Jimmy for lunch (dinner as we called it), and Mrs. Jessie had some packaged meat in the refrigerator and let us taste it. Oh my! It was good. It was bologna! We had never eaten or tasted any thing like that. We thought it was good, like candy!

I think it might have been when we were ages three to maybe nine years old when Mrs. Jessie and Mr. Jimmy started visiting us regularly. Mama always tried to have a very good dinner and Mrs. Jessie and Mr. Jimmy never failed to rave over the good food. It seems that they were not very familiar with our homemade cane syrup; at least, Mr. Jimmy was not. Nevertheless, Mama made wonderful and delicious biscuits with which we used to sop the syrup. They always visited us on Wednesday nights, and when possible, we saw them on Sundays.

I think it might have been during this time that my Daddy started fishing and peddling fish throughout the community to make a little extra money for the family. So, we had fish a lots when we had company.

My brother, sister, and I, as children, never noticed that Mr. Jimmy and Mrs. Jessie always came to see us on Christmas Eve night. As we grew older, we realized there was a reason; that was the night that Santa Claus came!. Maybe they were giving him a lift since they had the only vehicle in the community!

At the height of our friendship with Mr. Jimmy and Mrs. Jessie, we three children were so enthralled with all the stories and things they could tell us. One little song stands out to me. As I recall now, I can imagine Mrs. Jessie singing to us as we sat around her on the floor. She had a very outstanding singing voice and these are the words of the song that is so vivid in my mind today:

THREE LITTLE FISHIES (ITTY BITTY POOL)
Sung by Kay Kyser (#1 in 1939)
Words and music by Saxie Dowell

Down in the meadow in a little bitty pool
Swam three little fishies and a mama fishie too
"Swim" said the mama fishie, "Swim if you can"
And they swam and they swam all over the dam
Boop boop dittem dattem whattem Chu!
Boop boop dittem dattem whattem Chu!
Boop boop dittem dattem whattem Chu!
And they swam and they swam all over the dam
"Stop" said the mama fishie, "or you will get lost"

The three little fishies didn't wanna be bossed
The three little fishies went off on a spree
And they swam and they swam right out to the sea
Boop boop dittem dattem whattem Chu!
Boop boop dittem dattem whattem Chu!
Boop boop dittem dattem whattem Chu!
And they swam and they swam right out to the sea

And quick as they could; they turned on their tails
And back to the pool in the meadow they swam
And they swam and they swam back over the dam

Boop boop dittem dattem whattem Chu!
Boop boop dittem dattem whattem Chu!
Boop boop dittem dattem whattem Chu!
And they swam and they swam back over the dam.

Mrs. Jessie also went swimming with us many times in the creek behind the old grist mill near our home. (Fig. 27) We would have all day picnics there with them and other neighbors and friends. (Fig. 27A)

During these times we had traveling evangelists in this area. At one time Mr. Jimmy and Mrs. Jessie let, or maybe helped, an evangelist build a brush arbor on their property to use for revival meetings. One night Mr. Jimmy and Mrs. Jessie attended one of these services. It was quite a long sermon and Mr. Jimmy curled up on the bench, dozed off, and went to sleep. When he fell off the bench, the people in attendance thought he had received the Holy Spirit, and began to pray over him. He was astonished!

As all of us -- the Bells -- grew older, my brother went into the United States Air Force; I finished high school and took a job in Marianna as a stenographer; and Elaine finished high school and entered nursing school.

Mr. Jimmy, at this time, served as the substitute mail carrier in this area. He was very efficient and particular with this job. He told us he always waved each time he serviced a mailbox. Whether anyone was at home, he just waved to be sure.

Mr. Jimmy and Mrs. Jessie still visited in our home, and Mama and Daddy, also, visited them. The four of them discussed the opening of a restaurant or fish camp on Highway 2 near Neal's Landing. Daddy could furnish the fish, Mama could be a waitress along with Mrs. Jessie, and Mr. Jimmy could manage and tell interesting stories to the customers.

Well, close to the time of opening, Mr. Jimmy applied for the license. The first thing the State of Florida asked for was the blueprints of the building. Mr. Jimmy, as a self-taught draftsman himself, had drawn up the blueprints. They told him that he would have to be licensed for them to accept his own blueprints. He told them that he was as good as any licensed draftsman they had, but that was not good enough for the State of Florida. Mr. Jimmy said, "Okay, we do not have to open; we'll just close before we get started." He did just that. Mr. Jimmy did not like "government," and, especially, rules and regulations when he was "just trying to make a living."

He turned the restaurant into the museum over time. Sometime during this period, Mr. Jimmy and Mrs. Jessie's home burned, and they moved into the museum with the animals.

Fig. 27

Fig. 27a

CHAPTER XIX

When the house burned, many books were saved because Mr. Jimmy had built a special little house in the back of the home to store them. He had done this in order to have an extra bedroom in their home. When they moved to the museum, he built another little house in the rear of the museum for the books. The museum was just a little business to keep Mr. Jimmy busy and happy. He had, in the meantime, become interested in entomology. According to his diary, dated June 12, 1931, he said, "lately have been acquiring a renewed interest in entomology and it seems to be growing stronger each day."

You will note in the illustrations shown here (Fig. 28 thru 31) that he was accomplished in entomology. He often, in our presence, caught butterflies in the flower gardens he prepared for Mrs. Jessie. (Fig. 32) He would prepare the area and maybe plant the seed; however, Mrs. Jessie gave them the love and care they needed. He spent hours catching the butterflies with a net. Indeed, he knew the names of each one. Although, I never witnessed the process of saving the butterflies or preserving them I do remember Mr. Jimmy had many glass covered frames of different mounted butterflies inside. They were beautiful and hung in Mr. Jimmy and Mrs. Jessie's home.

He loved animals and had so many unusual ones; indeed, all kinds: snakes, three-toed sloths, anteaters, monkeys, and many more. (Fig. 33 thru 36a) He, himself, built all the pens, houses and cages for all of them. He could build almost anything he needed.

He built his own workshop on the museum property, where he did a lots of his plans and construction of different kinds. This building was the only building on the property that did not have a cement foundation. The museum was the home of unusual things and unusual animals, such as "Silvia" the python, so large it took both of them to pick her up and show her. The museum had lots of pictures of unusual-and please forgive me-freakish people that we might think of seeing at the early county fairs that we, at one time, had in this area. Mr. Jimmy and Mrs. Jessie both loved people and especially children, so they arranged for classes from the local schools to visit the museum for a very small fee.

Fig. 28

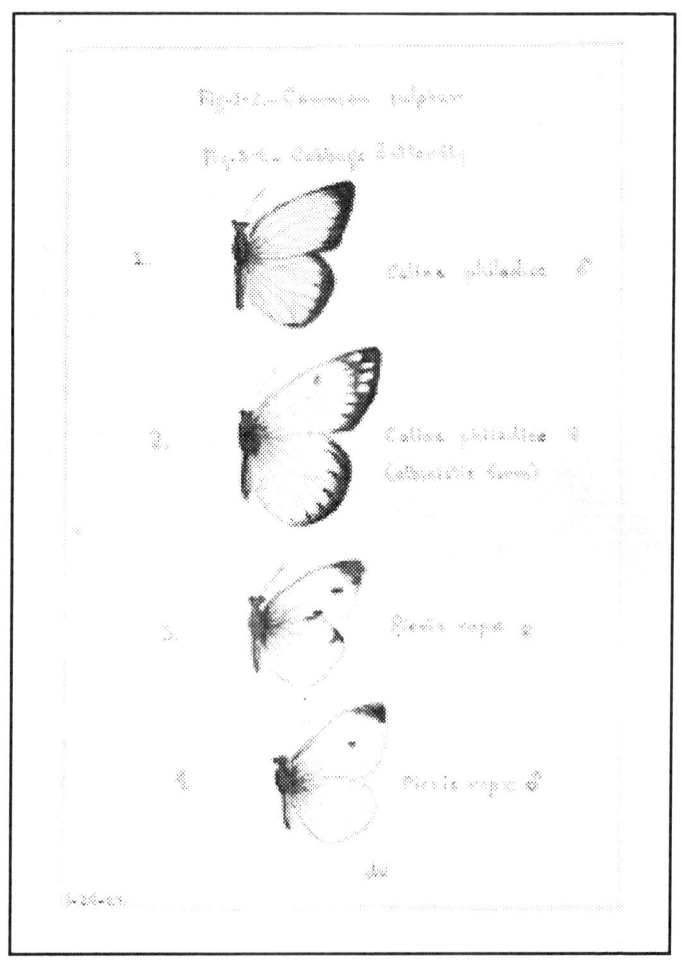
Fig. 1-2. Common sulphur
Fig. 3-4. Cabbage butterfly
1.
Colias philodice ♂
2.
Colias philodice ♀
(albinistic form)
3.
Pieris rapae ♀
4.
Pieris rapae ♂

Fig. 29

Fig. 30

Fig. 31

Fig. 32

Fig. 33

Fig. 34

Fig. 35

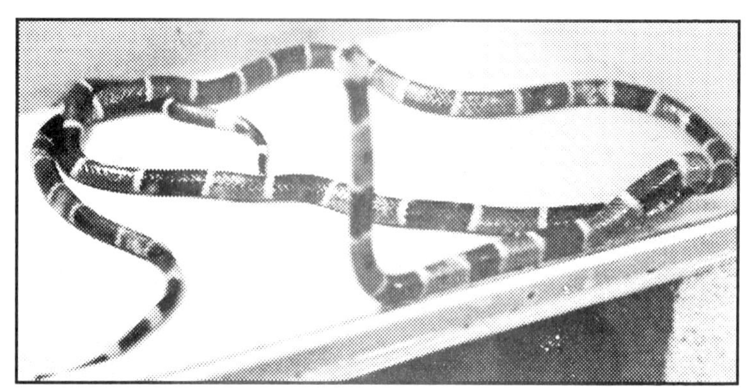

Fig. 36

Fig. 36a

CHAPTER XX

Mr. Jimmy was a person who always had projects. Perhaps, it was building Mrs. Jessie fancy flower gardens, planting vegetables or fruit trees, or, maybe, sometimes it was reading a new book.

At one time Mr. Jimmy went away for several weeks and studied electronics, refrigeration, and heating. I believe he studied in Chicago. Afterwards, he had a little radio shop in his yard across from the house. Many people, including friends and neighbors, brought their radios (if they were fortunate enough to have one) to be repaired or, maybe, to buy tubes for them. He had a very good little business. While operating this business he opened a little electronic shop in Malone, located behind Langston's Drug Store.

He enjoyed operating these shops because he loved people and company to talk with and discuss all things, including world affairs, politics, and anything else the people wanted to discuss. During this time there were people in our neighborhood that did not own a radio; thus meeting among neighbors and friends were frequent in order to listen to the news or stories on the radio.

The visitations between our families became less frequent due to their work. I believe Daddy, by this time was working other jobs but still trying to fish for a living. He used hoop nets for fishing, and he knitted and tarred them himself. Because of no refrigeration during this time, he built "live boxes," which were left in the Chattahoochee river to keep the fish fresh. When people came to purchase fish, my Daddy would go to the river and get fresh fish from the live boxes. Daddy, also, worked for a time at the shipyard in Panama City. Because of all this work, visitations with Mr. Jimmy and Mrs. Jessie were limited. Daddy, finally, went to work with the Corps of Engineers, U. S. Army, working on a snag boat, called the "Montgomery." They cleaned out the channel of the river from Apalachicola, Florida, to Columbus, Georgia. He worked on the Montgomery until his death in 1961, at age 52.

Although this story is written in honor of Mr. Jimmy and Mrs. Jessie, please indulge me, as a daughter devoted to her Father, in wishing to express my love to a wonderful man who died before he began to live.

CHAPTER XXI

Let me continue to talk about the museum: When Mr. Jimmy purchased the property, on which he built a building intended for a restaurant, there was a big wooden house on the property which he did not need and did not want. He allowed my Daddy to take the building down, and the lumber from that old house was used to build the "guest house," that sits in my yard today. (Fig. 37) My Daddy died before the building was finished.

On the property at the museum was an open well, which was probably used at one time for drinking water. Mr. Jimmy built it up as a wishing well, after opening the museum. Children and adults visited the museum and threw coins in the well. I assume those coins still remain in that old well.

Mr. Jimmy in 1969, about a year after Mrs. Jessie's death, donated 18,000 books to the Chipola Jr. College (now Chipola College) Library. There is an article printed in the Jackson County Floridan with reference to his gift. (Fig. 38)

At Mr. Jimmy's death, and by auction, my family purchased the remainder of his library. I always called Mr. Jimmy a self-taught genius.

Other than the article mentioned above there was no acknowledgement, however, thinking further about his gift and its meager acknowledgement, I somehow suspect Mr. Jimmy might have asked for no acknowledgement. He was the type of person that declined recognition for any good things he did; and he did many good things for many people.

Mr. Jimmy was always interested in the economy of our country. He was very busy with projects around the house, farming, and reading; however, he found time to write many letters to people in government, and other organizations concerning our economy. The following is a memo written in his own handwriting comparing the times of the Great Depression and the time he wrote this in January, 1969. (Fig. 38A)

Further writing about our economy. Mr. Jimmy, in March of 1968 wrote the following:

> "All Federal Reserve Notes which constitute most of our present currency, carry the in equivocal pledge that the United States "will pay to the bearer on demand" the number of dollars indicated. Instead of giving to the bearer on demand the dollars promised, the Treasury merely will give other paper promises to pay dollars. Such subterfuge, the substitution of promise for promise instead of the thing promised, is unworthy of a Great Nation and an Honest People."

Fig. 37

Private Book Collection Donated To Chipola Library

[illegible]

Roy Beall Sr. and Mrs. Eva J. Dixon examine some of the books from the James collection, that was recently donated to the CJC Library.

Fig. 38

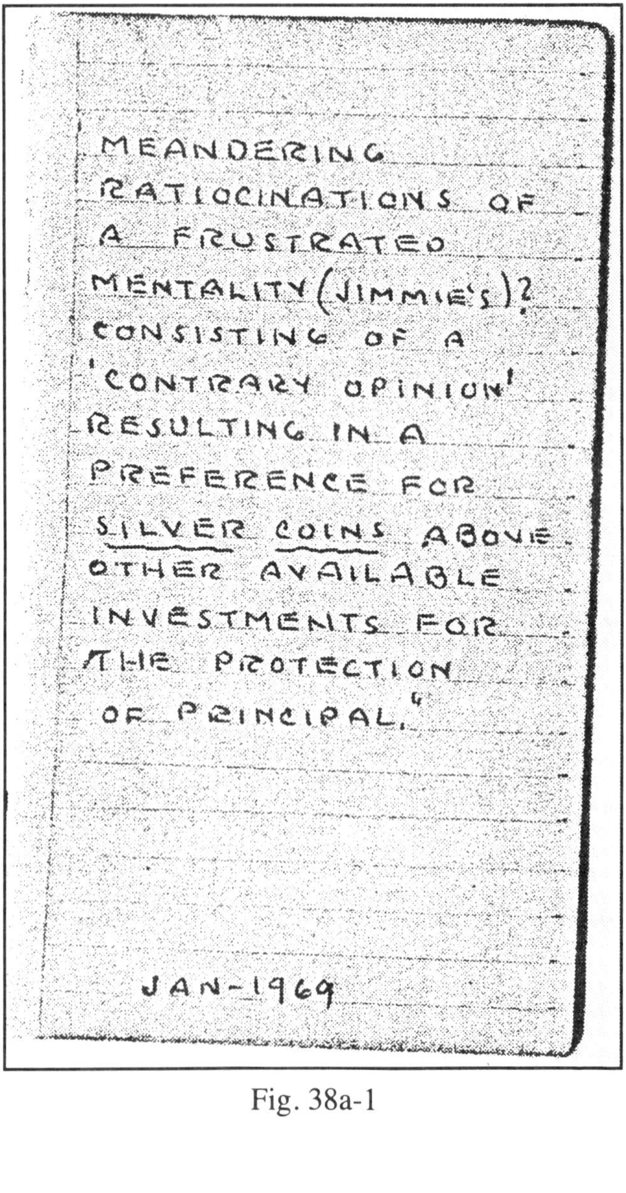

MEANDERING
RATIOCINATIONS OF
A FRUSTRATED
MENTALITY (JIMMIE'S)?
CONSISTING OF A
'CONTRARY OPINION'
RESULTING IN A
PREFERENCE FOR
<u>SILVER</u> <u>COINS</u> ABOVE
OTHER AVAILABLE
INVESTMENTS FOR
"THE PROTECTION
OF PRINCIPAL."

JAN-1969

Fig. 38a-1

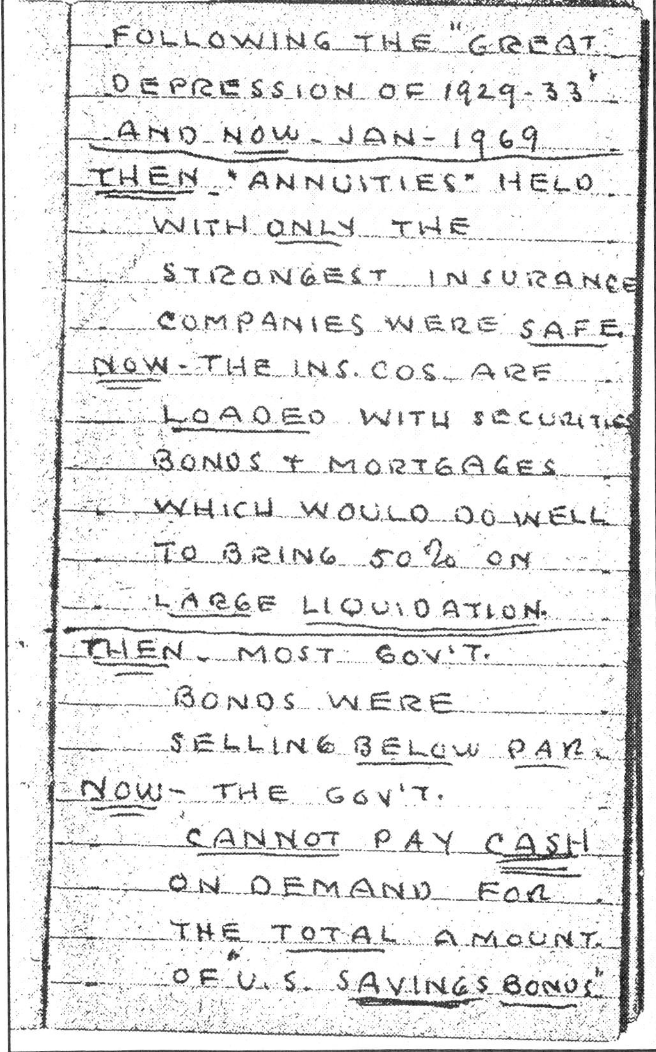

FOLLOWING THE "GREAT
DEPRESSION OF 1929-33"
AND NOW - JAN - 1969
THEN - "ANNUITIES" HELD
WITH ONLY THE
STRONGEST INSURANCE
COMPANIES WERE SAFE.
NOW - THE INS. COS. ARE
LOADED WITH SECURITIES
BONDS + MORTGAGES
WHICH WOULD DO WELL
TO BRING 50% ON
LARGE LIQUIDATION.
THEN - MOST GOV'T.
BONDS WERE
SELLING BELOW PAR.
NOW - THE GOV'T.
CANNOT PAY CASH
ON DEMAND FOR
THE TOTAL AMOUNT
OF U.S. SAVINGS BONDS

Fig. 38a-2

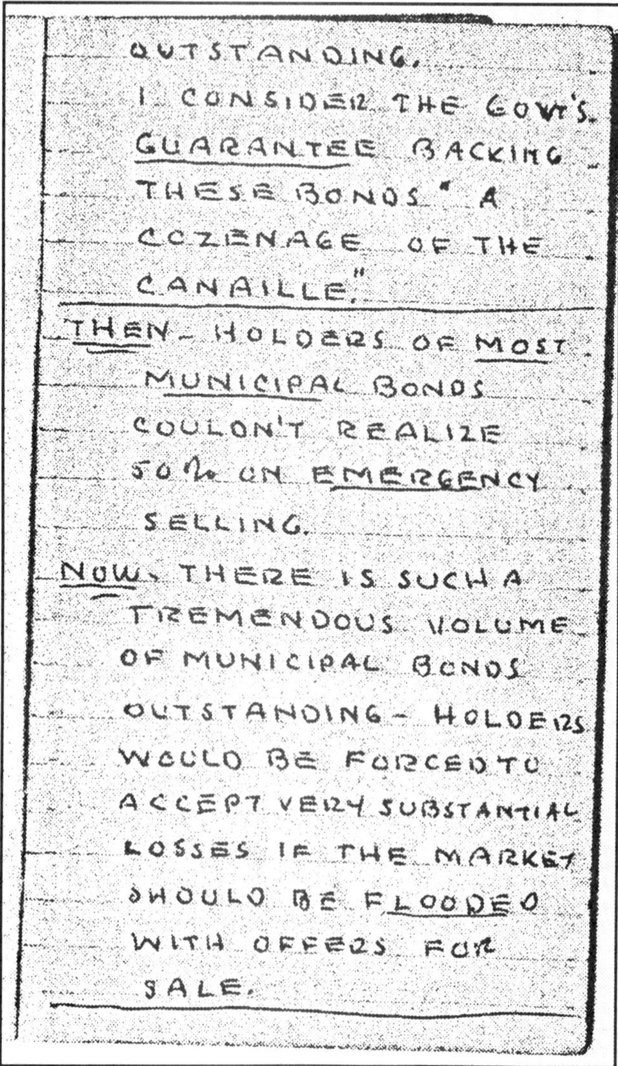

OUTSTANDING.
I CONSIDER THE GOV'T'S.
GUARANTEE BACKING
THESE BONDS " A
COZENAGE OF THE
CANAILLE."
THEN - HOLDERS OF MOST
MUNICIPAL BONDS
COULDN'T REALIZE
50% ON EMERGENCY
SELLING.
NOW, THERE IS SUCH A
TREMENDOUS VOLUME
OF MUNICIPAL BONDS
OUTSTANDING - HOLDERS
WOULD BE FORCED TO
ACCEPT VERY SUBSTANTIAL
LOSSES IF THE MARKET
SHOULD BE FLOODED
WITH OFFERS FOR
SALE.

Fig. 38a-3

THEN – THERE WERE –
GOLD AND SILVER
BULLION AND
COINS AVAILABLE –
NOW – U.S. MONEY IN
CIRCULATION CONSISTS
OF "FIAT PAPER CURRENCY"
AND MOSTLY "TOKEN" –
COINAGE – EXCEPT
"KENNEDY" HALVES –
OF 40% SILVER
(FORMER HALVES – 1964
AND BEFORE WERE
90% SILVER) – AND
IN ACCORDANCE WITH
"GRESHAM'S LAW" – MOST
OF THESE HALVES
ARE IMMEDIATELY
REMOVED FROM
CIRCULATION.
INCONVERTIBLE "FIAT"
PAPER MONEY IS

Fig. 38a-4

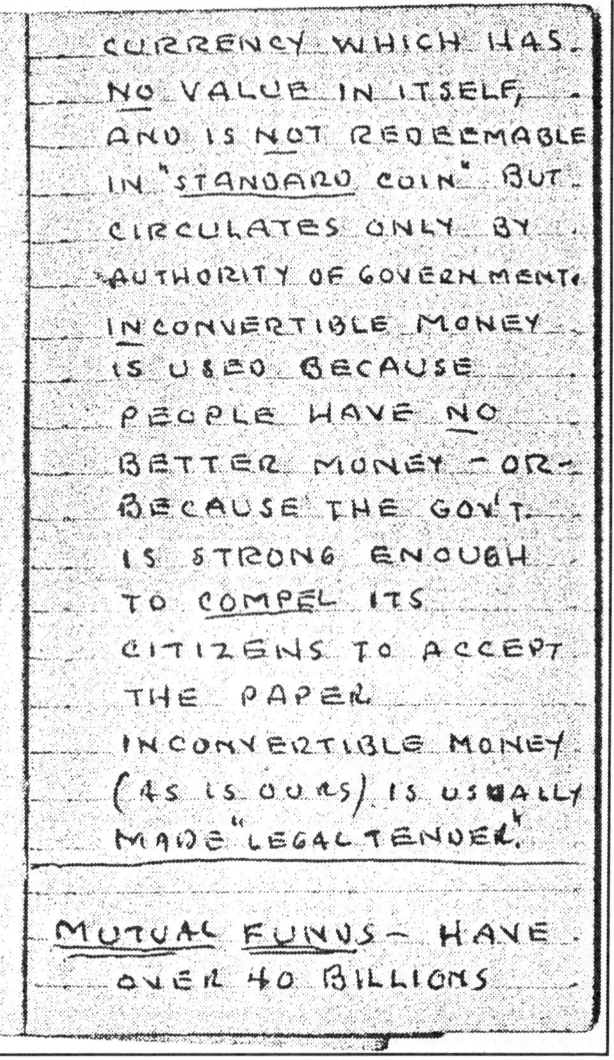
CURRENCY WHICH HAS
NO VALUE IN ITSELF,
AND IS NOT REDEEMABLE
IN "STANDARD COIN" BUT
CIRCULATES ONLY BY
AUTHORITY OF GOVERNMENT.
INCONVERTIBLE MONEY
IS USED BECAUSE
PEOPLE HAVE NO
BETTER MONEY - OR -
BECAUSE THE GOV'T.
IS STRONG ENOUGH
TO COMPEL ITS
CITIZENS TO ACCEPT
THE PAPER.
INCONVERTIBLE MONEY
(AS IS OURS) IS USUALLY
MADE "LEGAL TENDER".

MUTUAL FUNDS - HAVE
OVER 40 BILLIONS

Fig. 38a-5

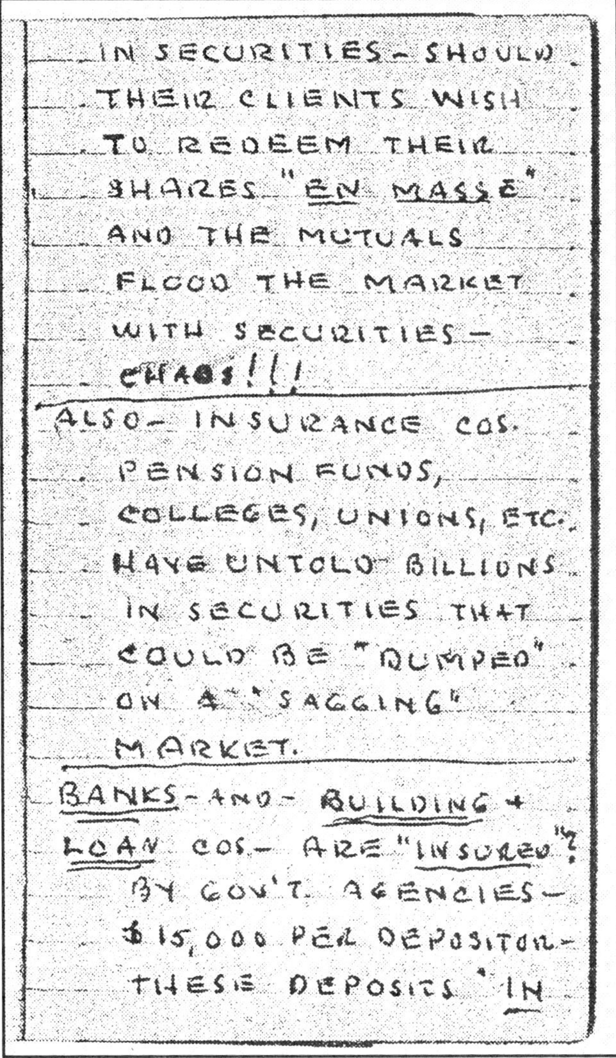

IN SECURITIES – SHOULD
THEIR CLIENTS WISH
TO REDEEM THEIR
SHARES "EN MASSE"
AND THE MUTUALS
FLOOD THE MARKET
WITH SECURITIES –
CHAOS!!!

ALSO – INSURANCE COS.
PENSION FUNDS,
COLLEGES, UNIONS, ETC.
HAVE UNTOLD BILLIONS
IN SECURITIES THAT
COULD BE "DUMPED"
ON A "SAGGING"
MARKET.

BANKS – AND – BUILDING +
LOAN COS. – ARE "INSURED"?
BY GOV'T. AGENCIES –
$15,000 PER DEPOSITOR –
THESE DEPOSITS "IN

Fig. 38a-6

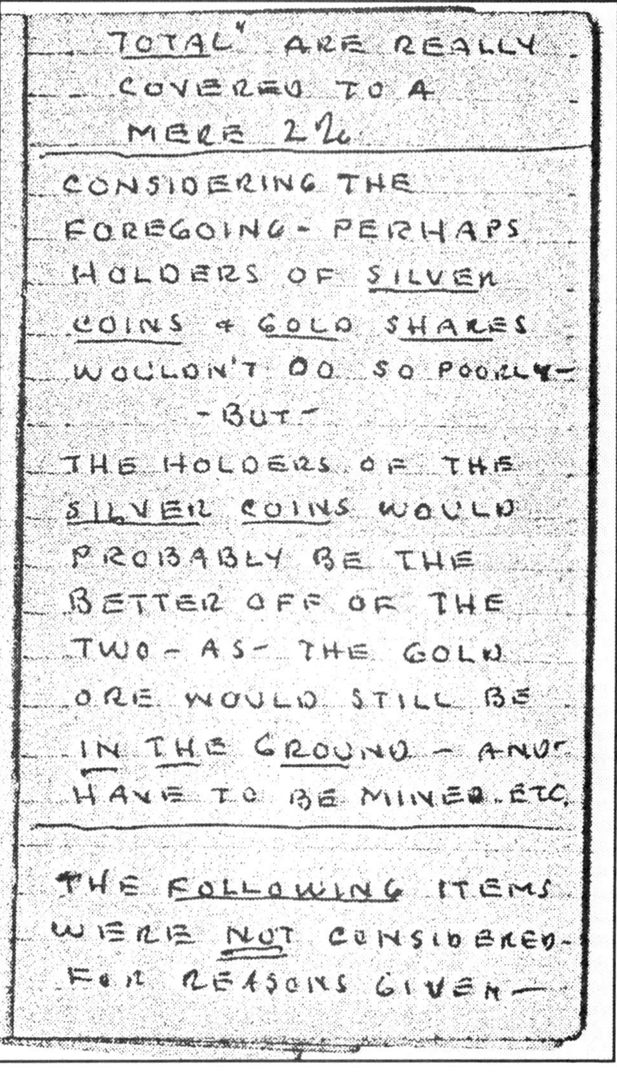

TOTAL' ARE REALLY
COVERED TO A
MERE 2%

CONSIDERING THE
FOREGOING - PERHAPS
HOLDERS OF SILVER
COINS & GOLD SHARES
WOULDN'T DO SO POORLY -
- BUT -
THE HOLDERS OF THE
SILVER COINS WOULD
PROBABLY BE THE
BETTER OFF OF THE
TWO - AS - THE GOLD
ORE WOULD STILL BE
IN THE GROUND - AND
HAVE TO BE MINED ETC.

THE FOLLOWING ITEMS
WERE NOT CONSIDERED -
FOR REASONS GIVEN -

Fig. 38a-7

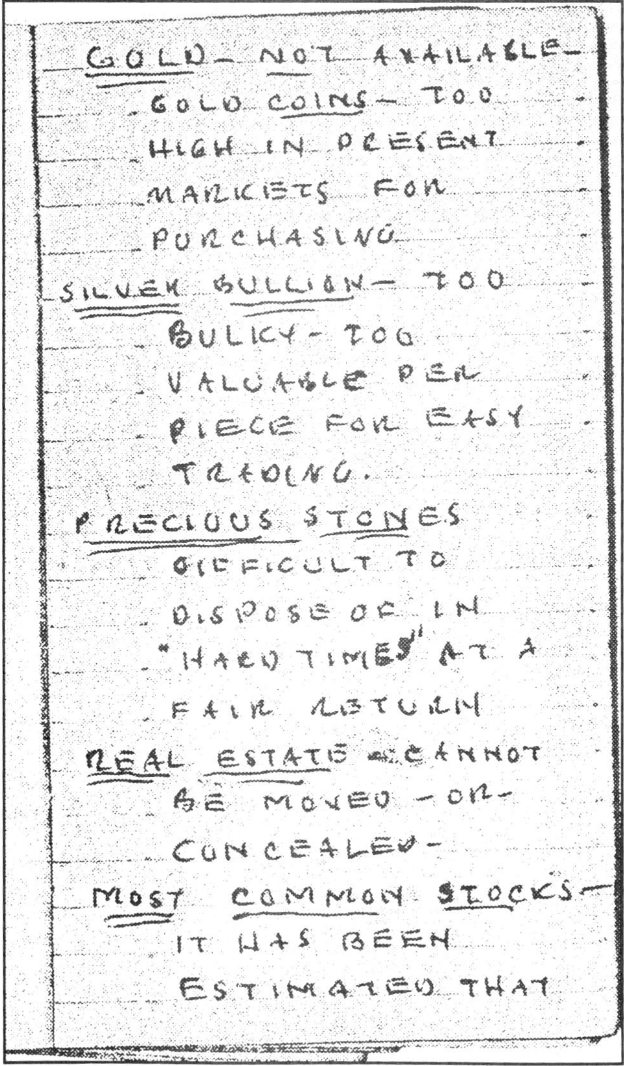
GOLD – NOT AVAILABLE –
GOLD COINS – TOO
HIGH IN PRESENT
MARKETS FOR
PURCHASING
SILVER BULLION – TOO
BULKY – TOO
VALUABLE PER
PIECE FOR EASY
TRADING.
PRECIOUS STONES
DIFFICULT TO
DISPOSE OF IN
"HARD TIMES" AT A
FAIR RETURN
REAL ESTATE – CANNOT
BE MOVED – OR –
CONCEALED –
MOST COMMON STOCKS –
IT HAS BEEN
ESTIMATED THAT

Fig. 38a-8

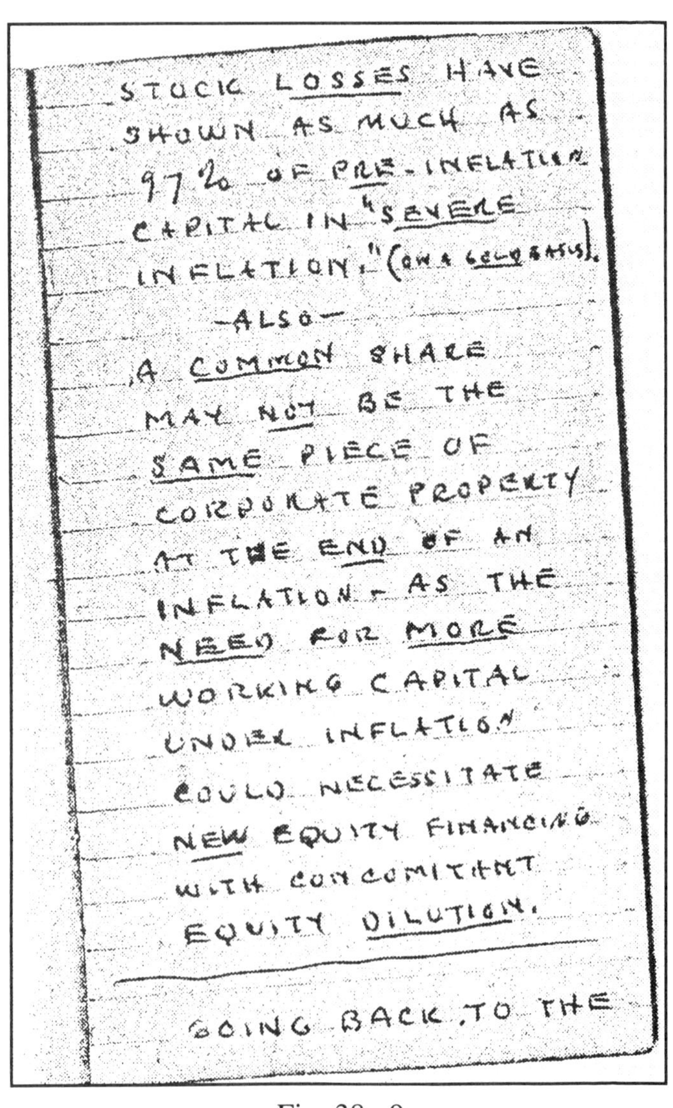
STOCK LOSSES HAVE
SHOWN AS MUCH AS
97% OF PRE-INFLATION
CAPITAL IN "SEVERE
INFLATION." (ON A GOLD BASIS).

—ALSO—

A COMMON SHARE
MAY NOT BE THE
SAME PIECE OF
CORPORATE PROPERTY
AT THE END OF AN
INFLATION — AS THE
NEED FOR MORE
WORKING CAPITAL
UNDER INFLATION
COULD NECESSITATE
NEW EQUITY FINANCING
WITH CONCOMITANT
EQUITY DILUTION.

GOING BACK TO THE

Fig. 38a-9

WORST BEAR MARKET OF THEM ALL - 1929-32 - THE MOST STAGGERING LOSSES WERE INCURRED NOT IN THE INITIAL CRASH ITSELF BUT IN THE PREMATURE "BARGAIN" BUYING THEREAFTER.

UNDER INFLATION THE STRONGEST INSTRUMENTS ARE OFTEN THE WEAKEST AND THE WEAKEST ARE THE BEST.

BONDS, BANK ACCOUNTS, AND LIFE INSURANCE BECOME ENDOWED WITH A HIGH DEGREE OF SPECULATIVE RASH. THE SAFER MORE SOLID THE INSTRUMENT, THE MORE SURELY WILL A RISING COST OF LIVING REDUCE ITS BUYING POWER.

TO THE EXTENT TO WHICH MONEY IS WANTED BECAUSE OF ITS DESIRABILITY AS BULLION IT MUST BE ONSIDERE WEALTH.

Fig. 38a-10

CHAPTER XXII

Mrs. Jessie died sometime around July 31, 1968. (She was born August 3, 1903.) She was in the hospital at Donalsonville, Georgia. I'm under the impression and believe it was a problem concerning severe headaches maybe a brain tumor or something similar. I never saw the death certificate.

I will tell you, dear reader, that at the time they were working as aerialists and performing their daring acts, Mrs. Jessie fell from the high wire. From the time I remember seeing Mrs. Jessie, she had a knot on her forehead about the size of an acorn. During her later years she had the knot removed. Often in our presence she complained of headaches. Whether this had anything to do with her death, I do not know; however, I've often wondered about it. (Fig. 39)

Mr. Jimmy told the funeral director to put her in the finest casket and dress her as if it were his own mother. He viewed the body and had the casket sealed ,refusing anyone else to view. She then was taken to another town in Georgia to be cremated since there was not a crematory nearby. Before reaching the crematory, they were stopped because someone in her family, I'm not sure who had complained and alleged that Mr. Jimmy had poisoned her. There was a court order issued on this alleged complaint. Consequently, there was an autopsy performed. Nothing was found. Mr. Jimmy was very upset about this incident, understanding what is necessary to be done to a body when an autopsy is performed. Mr. Jimmy never forgave nor had anything to do with the people he believed responsible for this.

Now I'd like to point out that at this time, Mrs. Jessie's sister, Ruth Bender, who still visited Mr. Jimmy, never believed Mr. Jimmy would harm Mrs. Jessie.

Mrs. Jessie had a flower house in the back of the museum where there were neatly built houses and pens for the animals. Mrs. Jessie's flower house was a special place because much love and patience was spent by Mr. Jimmy in building it for Mrs. Jessie. Mr. Jimmy buried Mrs. Jessie (her ashes) inside the front of the flower house. He told us he would be buried in the back of the house; in other words, he was not as deserving as Mrs. Jessie.

Shortly after Mrs. Jessie's death, Mr. Jimmy wrote a "Remembrance of the love expressed by Mrs. Jessie." It was written and dated July 31, 1968, at 1:15 A.M. (Fig. 40)

Fig. 39

"MY JESSIE"

NURSE ELIZABETH ROGERS TOLD ME THE LAST THING DR. HOLLEY EVER HEARD JESSIE SAY WAS—

"JIMMIE HAS BEEN WONDERFUL TO ME."

SHORTLY BEFORE I LOST HER JESS SAID TO ME—

"MARRYING YOU WAS THE BEST THING I EVER DID IN MY WHOLE LIFE."

JULY-31-1968- 1.15 AM.- EST.

Fig. 40

CHAPTER XXIII

Ten years later in 1978, it was a beautiful spring day; insects were buzzing, butterflies were fluttering, and sunlight was blazing upon the newly planted zinnias that Mr. Jimmy had purchased a few days ago. This pathetic and forlorn human being, Mr. Jimmy, had arisen that glorious morning to experience that magnificent vista.

In his heart, he knew that this majesty of nature would be his last remembrance of beauty on this plane of existence. However, in his last breath of mortality, he knew there was one person who must be given respect and love before his final departure from life. In loving adoration, he approached the ashen remains of his beloved Jessie in the flower house that he had built for her many years ago. He uttered a vow of love and praise to her.

Slowly, with solemn deliberation, Mr. Jimmy approached his automobile, which was parked behind his building of residence and business. He knew what was necessary; and he had made all of the provisions for this last endeavor. Poison gas had been purchased several days prior to this suicidal venture. Without hesitation or remorse, he entered his vehicle. After closing the doors, he turned on the poisonous gases, committing his existence to the all-consuming finality of death.

How sad it was! He was a magnificent man with such great potential. How could he, of all people, forget about the spiritual consequences of taking his own. life? (Suicide is an act that is completely incomprehensible to most people; but it does occur with frightful frequency.)

Perhaps, Mr. Jimmy, embracing the beliefs of the agnostic that he was, did not even dwell upon the question of right or wrong.

It is not my intention to judge Mr. Jimmy's actions. He was a spiritual being as are we all. His actions are judged by a power far greater than any of us. To this omniscient deity, we commit his spirit and pray for mercy upon his soul. This same prayer is offered to every other human being who has lived and died. God's judgment is not limited to Mr. Jimmy; it is the ultimate fate of everyone who has ever existed.

CHAPTER XXIV

Yes, Mr. Jimmy and Mrs. Jessie were two amazing individuals whose exploits were far "above the crowd" in every sense of the expression. I have striven to present them in a light that illuminates their extraordinary talents and strengths, yet concedes their weaknesses and faults. In this endeavor I hope that I have succeeded. Furthermore, may this literary presentation be a source of enjoyment and information to you, dear reader and friend.

After a few days of not picking up his mail from his box in front of the museum where he lived (although he did not operate the museum), the mail carrier called Mrs. Ruth, who was Mrs. Jessie's sister. She came to our home and told my Mother. (Fig. 41)

Mama got in touch with my sister, Elaine, who lived in a mobile home in the yard. She and a friend, Sylvia, immediately went to the museum and searched for quite a while before finding the body in his car. My Mama in the meantime called my brother and he came to the museum also. After finding Mr. Jimmy and knowing he was deceased, they came back to Mama's home and told Mrs. Ruth that he was gone. The authorities were called at that time. My family returned to the museum to be present when the authorities arrived.

They were there when the car was opened and their account of the situation went something like this: initially, through the windows Mr. Jimmy just looked like he was asleep. However, when the doors were opened and the air hit him, his body turned completely black. They were so aghast with their findings that they reeled backward and shuddered in horror!

From that day forward his estate was handled by the named personal representative with the assistance of an attorney. This estate is public record in the Circuit Court of Jackson County, Florida. Mr. Jimmy left in his safe deposit box his Will along with a sealed envelope which read, "To be opened only in the presence of a Salvation Army officer." When this envelope was opened in the presence of a Salvation Army officer, it told the directions as to where his precious coins were located. The authorities followed the directions and found the coins underneath his work shop which did not have a cement floor (as I have stated before in this story). Mr. Jimmy had dug out a space large enough to place all of his coins in five-gallon buckets. He had many uncirculated coins, gold and silver, located in the space provided.

When the estate was closed and the museum and the acreage around it was sold, we became concerned about Mrs. Jessie's ashes. Therefore; my brother with much uneasiness went to the personal representative and expressed his concern. He was told that the ashes could not be found. My brother went to the flower house and found the ashes of Mrs. Jessie. He took them to the personal representative and asked if the Salvation Army could, at least, bury them. As far as I know, Mr. Jimmy's ashes had never been buried. I presume the funeral director was still in possession of them.

Mr. Jimmy and Mrs. Jessie were buried in the Bazzell Cemetery, which is located at the very end of Timberlane Road in the Lovedale community. Permission was given to bury them at this location by the directors of the cemetery. The Salvation Army was left all the assets of the estate. The burial and headstones placed at the site were handled by the personal representative of the estate and/or the Salvation Army. (Fig. 42)

Fig. 41

Fig. 42

CHAPTER XXV

Even though this is the story of Mrs. Jessie and Mr. Jimmy, there is someone that Charles and I feel must be acknowledged because he has decided to contribute to this literary work and because of his magnificent stature among the people of this community.

Mr. Virgil Oswald has given in time and effort so much to so many people that he has become somewhat iconic to the myriad people who know, appreciate, and love him. He is indeed, a person who has gained the acclaim and respect that accompanies goodness and great accomplishments.

We honor Mr. Oswald and proudly offer the following anecdotal information afforded by him in his own words:

"When I was a small child, I remember my mother telling me about the Frog Man, after she had seen the Mighty Haag Circus in Marianna. Mr. Jimmy Walters was the Frog Man and according to her, he was the highlight of the show. The antics that he displayed were very funny and amusing.

"On another occasion when the Mighty Haag Show played in Malone, my brother James and I wanted to attend but we didn't have the twenty-five cents admission charge. We contacted a neighbor who wanted a tree on his property cut and sawed into firewood. We did the job for him, and he paid us twenty-five cents each. We went to the circus, saw Jimmy and Jessie perform, and enjoyed it immensely.

"When I was in Third Grade in Malone School, I vividly remember this happening: The circus traveled from their winter home in Marianna to Malone for an afternoon and evening performance. At that time the road from Marianna came directly by the school building. The teachers allowed the students to go to the windows and watch the passing parade. First came the slow-moving trucks carrying equipment and supplies with show personnel. Then came the caged animal wagons with the three elephants and camel on foot. That was the first treat of the day. Then the teacher allowed a group of us students to go to town during the one hour lunch period to watch the tent raising. We had the time of our lives and were a little late returning to school. The teacher was not happy about that.

"At another time when the Mighty Haag played in Malone, quite a commotion happened after the circus performance ended and the audience was leaving the tent. It seems that a fellow in quite an inebriated condition had enjoyed the show between sips of liquor. He was in no form of acceptable behavior and was 'raising Cain.' A 'gun-happy' deputy trying to take control of the situation, shot his pistol into the air. You can imagine what this did to the crowd- bedlam! The drunk man ran in among the three elephants as they were being led from the tent. When he realized where he was, he loudly called out for his wife in excitement, 'Bessie, come here!' He then ran wildly in the opposite direction and as he approached the lion's cage, the lion let out a vicious roar. All he could do then was to jump up and down and call Bessie. His wife soon found him and took him home.

"When I was in Junior High School, I had classes with James and Louise Keith. They were nephew and niece of Mrs. Jessie. When the Mighty Haag played in Malone that year, the show paraded the streets in advertising the afternoon and evening performances. During a recess period the parade came by the school building, and Louise ran out to the edge of the street. The vehicle carrying Mrs. Jessie stopped, Louise and Jessie embraced, and the vehicle continued on its way. Then Louise returned to our group gushing with pride. We were all astonished to know that Louise and James were related to one of the stars of the show."

CHAPTER XXVI

ANECDOTES

Many years ago, this story was told to me and I thought it was rather funny. When W. H. was living with Aunt Annie Pyke Ford, he was very observant about things going on around him. Aunt Annie was a good seamstress and made most of the girls' clothing. One day she was making brassieres for the four girls and she noticed W.H. was over in the corner of the room and he was crying and whining. Asking him what was wrong, he replied, "I want you to make me a 'zeer' too."

* *

This is a revelation related to me many years ago, although, I do not know by whom. Mrs. Jessie, while working as a waitress in Marianna, and at the time she met Mr. Jimmy, was very poor, regarding material things. She had only one slip (underwear) and each night she laundered that slip, in order that she might have it for the next day. This lack of material things might have had some bearing on her decision to go with Mr. Jimmy.

* *

Once when Mr. Jimmy and Mrs. Jessie visited Mrs. Annie Pyke Ford and W. H., a funny incident happened. All the men were outside the house at the tobacco barn. When they arrived, Mr. Jimmy went in the house and sat down in a chair and being so short, his feet did not touch the floor. He arose from the chair, picked the chair up and took it outside.

When he returned with the chair, he set the chair down and sat in it saying, "Now my feet will touch the floor." He had sawed off the legs and made them shorter so his feet would reach the floor. Charles and Luree Hudson told this to me recently when I contacted them about this book.

* *

Herman Laramore related a story about the Splendid Cafe in Marianna. (Please remember, this was the cafe once operated by Tommy Saliba, on Constitution Lane.)

Herman's Father was doing a construction job near the cafe, but across the busy street. Herman being a small boy at that time, just tagging along with his Dad, was very careful in getting across the street. He had eighty-nine cents in his pocket and he was very hungry. He entered the Splendid Cafe. He had never been in a restaurant before. However, he sat down and ordered fried chicken. He says he ate a whole chicken that day.

* *

In a conversation with Robert Allen. Peeler from Malone, Florida, who happens to be a very good friend of both me and my husband, he related several things he remembered about Mr. Jimmy and Mrs. Jessie.

His first recollection and statement to me was, "They were some of the very finest people I have ever known."

He recalls that they had a fire at the museum on one of the coldest nights he can remember. The call came into the Malone Fire Department (volunteer department) after dark. The fire department truck went to the fire, but the pump was frozen and they could not get water.

It happened that Robert Allen owned a fire truck and he was called. He and Bozo, a black man whom he employed, set out to the fire and found that the fire had started in the area where the animals were kept in freezing weather. The fire was still burning.

Robert Allen and Bozo brought in the ladder, and Bozo climbed the ladder to the top of the building. As he was climbing the ladder, he kept saying to Robert Allen, "Man, don't keep pushing me."

(Let me say at this point that Mrs. Jessie had met Robert Allen at the door, and she was crying and asking him to please save her anteater.) Robert Allen answered Bozo in this manner, "Man, I'm not pushing you; I'm on the floor."

At that time Bozo turned around, and, realizing that it was the anteater pushing him, he jumped off the ladder and landed on the floor with the anteater. Robert Allen grabbed the anteater and handed him to Mrs. Jessie and she wrapped him in a blanket.

They tried to get into another room and found all the snakes crawling around on the floor.

Robert Allen went to Mrs. Jessie and said, "I'm sorry, but we can't go in there with all of those poisonous snakes." Mrs. Jessie immediately picked up a rake and began to rake them out. Some of them were blistered from the fire and had to be euthanized. Mrs. Jessie said to Robert Allen, "I had to release the snakes from the cages because I could not let them die in captivity." The next morning Robert Allen said they were at his door and paid him for his services.

It was determined that the cause of the fire was as follows: Because of such cold weather, Mr. Jimmy had filled buckets with coal and set them around the rooms to keep the animals warm. One of the animals (probably, the anteater, which was one of the largest animals in that room) turned over one of the buckets of coal and thereby started the fire.

* *

In speaking with Leo "Robbie" Robinson by phone with reference to Mr. Jimmy and Mrs. Jessie, he told me this Story.

He and his two brothers, C. H. and Brantley, lived with their widowed mother in a little house next door to Mr. Jimmy and Mrs. Jessie. They were poor like my family. The difference however was they had no father to make a living for them. And so, the boys had to make a living for the family.

Their mother was a good woman with no education and with no way to bring in the bread. They were destitute and there was no one to direct them in a way to get help (we would, in this era, call it welfare). The boys had to work with farmers in the fields for whatever they would pay them. All of their money, which was very little, was spent for groceries and necessities.

Mr. Jimmy asked Leo if he would gather the eggs under the barn, and if he would do so, the family could have the eggs. Gladly, Leo's mother accepted the offer because they needed the eggs.

Leo says he was scared to death to crawl under the barn, but he did it many, many, times to please his mother and Mr. Jimmy, and specially to feed the family.

Leo told me that he was probably in the home of Mr. Jimmy and Mrs. Jessie, maybe, twice. Why? He says he felt inferior because of his family's financial situation; although, Mr. Jimmy and Mrs. Jessie were always nice to him.

Incidentally, neither Leo nor his brothers, were able to attend school very much because of the situation of having to work for a living at such a young age.

When we visited Mr. Jimmy and Mrs. Jessie, we would go down and get Leo and his brothers and they would come up to Mr. Jimmy's house and play with us in the yard.

When Leo grew up, he married Ruth Jordan, joined the United States Air Force, had a lovely family and now has grandchildren and great grandchildren. He retired from the United States Air force, worked at another job in Ohio for many years. And he now lives a comfortable life in Ohio where most of his children have settled.

****

Aaron (Billy) McAllister came by a few minutes one day and we discussed several things. I asked him what he could remember about Mr. Jimmy and Mrs. Jessie. He related to me that he did remember them but knew very little about them.

But then he recalled that one day he and a friend were going fishing at Neal's Landing early in the morning. As they passed the museum, they noticed a black man in a truck stopped in front of the museum. It was the same man who had knocked down the mailbox belonging to Mr. Jimmy. After they thought about it, they decided to go back and tell Mr. Jimmy of the incident so he could maybe call the authorities. This incident happened to be the same year that he had lost Mrs. Jessie. They tried to tell Mr. Jimmy what had happened. However, Mr. Jimmy wrongly thought, since the black man was no longer there, that Billy and his friend had damaged his box and had come back to tell him that someone else had damaged the box.

They never could convince Mr. Jimmy that they were only trying to help him.

****

EPILOGUE

The dawn breaks and the sun rises, heralding the beginning of a new majestic awakening. Maybe, life is akin to such happenings. Like the sun that proclaims the genesis of a new day without any constraints or promises, our lives are initiated and terminated in a similar fashion. We are born; we live; we die -- so simple, so definite.

So were our heroes, Mr. Jimmy and Mrs. Jessie. Their lives were a culmination of many elements welded together in an expression that was unique and unforgettable.

In the beginning, I expressed my love and adoration for Mr. Jimmy and Mrs. Jessie; what more can I say about them in the ending? Perhaps, just a fond farewell might suffice; or maybe, as the French might say, "*Bon voyage!*" "*Je t'adore, mes amis.*" "*Au revoir.*"

Yes, in French, every utterance sounds significant and exciting. However, the English translation bespeaks of wishes of good fortune in the beginning, and then expresses loving friendship and, finally, farewell.

So, just as "farewell" becomes "*au revoir*" in French, "goodbye" becomes the ending in our literary stroll down memory lane with Mr. Jimmy and Mrs. Jessie.

INDEX OF CHARACTERS

(Listed Alphabetically)

Allen, Miss
Bazzell, Laura
Beall, Roy
Bell, Charles
Bell, Charlie
Bell, Elaine
Bell, Johnnie Ford
Bender, Harry
Bender, Ruth
Byrd, Admiral
Corcoran, J. C.
Dietrich, Marlene
Ford, Annie Pyke
Ford, Annie Ross (Hodges)
Ford, Inez (Hudson)
Ford, Mary Lizzie (Owens)
Ford, Maude (Stephens)
Gauger, Ruth
Haag, Ernest
Haag, Widow of Ernest
Haag, Harry
Heald, Tee
Hill, Ruby
Hodges, Tee
Hudson, Charles
Hudson, Luree
Hutchins, Sylvia
James, Jessie
James, John F. (Pop)
James, Leon K.
James, Stella Klein
Keith, Andrew J.
Keith, Beulah
Keith, Cora Johnson
Keith, Douglas
Keith, Edell (Coleman)
Keith, Evelyn (Baxter)
Keith, James
Keith, Junior
Keith, Louise (Woodham)
Keith, Martha Hawthorne
Keith, Minnie (Pittman)
Keith, Reuben
Keith, Robert
Keith, Will
Keith, Willie Pearl (Conrad)
King, Charles
King, Clarice
King, J. D.
King, Lillian (Sasnett)
King, Louise (Yatauro)
Laramore, Herman
Macklin, Nancy
McAllister, Aaron (Billy)
McIntyre, Paul
Mix, Tom
Mosely, Dr.
Oswald, Virgil
Padgett, Rex
Peeler, Robert Allen
Pyke, Lucy
Pyke, Rhoda Elizabeth
Pyke, W. H., Sr.
Pyke, W. H., Jr.
Pyke, William H. (W.H.)
Robinson, Leo (Robbie)
Robinson, Ruth
Rogers, Elizabeth
Saliba, Tee
Saliba, Tommy
Smuck, Guy
Strickland, Harmon
Strickland, Mary.
Walters, Ernest (Bozo)
Walters, James
Walters, Jessie
Walters, Jimmy
Wilkinson, Carlos
Wilkinson, Catherine